AF406543

How Can I Trust You Again?

A Step-by-Step Guide to Rebuilding Trust After Infidelity

Jeffrey D. Murrah

Restore The Family Press

Copyright © 2012 by Jeffrey D. Murrah

All rights reserved.

No portion of this book may be reproduced in any form without written permission from the publisher or author, except as permitted by U.S. copyright law.

Contents

Chapter One

What is Trust?

A Foundation Shaken

When an affair rocks your marriage, it shatters the very foundation of your relationship – trust. That unshakeable confidence you once had in your spouse is now in pieces, leaving you questioning everything. Can you ever trust them again? Should you? Once trust is broken, can it ever be repaired?

There's no sugarcoating it – infidelity is a devastating betrayal that turns your world upside down. Suddenly, those simple everyday interactions with your spouse that you never gave a second thought to are now fraught with doubt and suspicion. When they say they're running out for an errand, can you believe them? When they come home late from work, are they really where they say they were? The uncertainty is maddening. Your mind imagines the worst.

Imagine this scenario: Your spouse tells you they must work late tonight. Before the affair, you wouldn't have thought twice about it. But now, your mind races with questions. Are they really at the office, or are they sneaking off to meet their affair partner? Are they lying to you again, just like they did before? The seed of doubt has been planted and grows each minute they're not home.

Or perhaps you're the one who strayed and are desperately trying to regain your spouse's trust. You've cut off all contact with your affair partner, you're being completely transparent with your phone and email, and you're doing everything you can to prove your commitment to your marriage. But your spouse still looks at you with wary eyes, questioning your every move. You feel like you're walking on eggshells, never knowing what will trigger their suspicion or anger. The weight of your betrayal hangs heavy between you.

Of course, you desperately want to trust your spouse again or to be trusted by them. You long for that peace of mind and security you once had, to be free from the constant anxiety and second-guessing. But when trust has been broken like this, it cannot be easily repaired with an apology and a promise. There's no quick-fix solution. Rebuilding trust after an affair is a long and difficult journey that both partners must be fully committed to.

So, where do you even begin?

The first step is understanding what trust really is. We often throw around the word "trust" without fully grasping its meaning and implications. Trust is a complex concept that can take different forms:

- As a noun, trust is the firm belief in someone's reliability and integrity. It's a bond of honesty and dependability.

- As a verb, trust is the action of placing your confidence in someone, even without concrete proof. It's giving them the benefit of the doubt.

Interestingly, the verb "trust" can be used in two different ways – transitively and intransitively. Using transitively means you're trusting a specific person or thing. For example, "I trust my spouse to be faithful." When used intransitively, it refers to the general state of being trusting. For instance, "After the affair, I find it hard to trust."

These subtle variations in meaning are important because they change the very nature of what you're talking about when you say "trust." It's easy for the message to get lost in translation between partners. When your unfaithful spouse says, "Have a little trust in me," what are they really asking for? Blind faith in their word? Exasperation that you no longer trust them? A second chance to prove their trustworthiness through action? Understanding their true intent requires open and honest communication and asking hard questions.

There's no other way around it – for a marriage to heal from infidelity, you need to rediscover and redefine what trust means for you as a couple. It starts with looking inward and articulating what you each need to feel trust and safety in the relationship again. You need courage in asking and answering challenging questions. For the betrayed partner, that might mean full transparency, remorse, and consistent, trustworthy behavior over time from the unfaithful spouse. For the unfaithful partner, it might mean being allowed to demonstrate their commitment to change and make amends. You can't just fall back into old patterns and toxic dynamics and expect trust to reappear.

This is where both partners need to be fully on board. Rebuilding trust is a two-way street that requires effort, patience, and vulnerability from both sides. The betrayed spouse needs to be willing to risk trusting again and slowly let their guard down as their partner proves their trustworthiness. The unfaithful spouse needs to be unflinchingly honest, accountable, and patient, understanding that regaining trust will take time and there will be setbacks along the way. Both partners must be committed to showing up and doing the work, even when it's painful and difficult.

Learning to trust again is a gradual process of reopening your heart, one small step at a time, as your spouse earns back your trust through their actions, not just their words. It's a dance of vulnerability and risk, fear and faith. But as difficult as it is, restoring trust is possible when you're both willing to show up with humility, empathy, and steadfast commitment to each other.

Ultimately, rebuilding trust is about so much more than getting back to where you were before the affair. It's an opportunity to create something even stronger and more authentic. By facing this ultimate test of your bond and rediscovering what trust and commitment truly mean to you, you can emerge with a deeper level of intimacy, understanding, and appreciation for each other. A love that has been shattered and put back together is a love that can withstand anything.

TRUST EXERCISE:

- What does it mean to you to trust someone? What makes someone worthy of your trust?

- What actions and qualities do you need to see in your spouse to feel safe trusting again?

- What does your spouse need from you to rebuild their trust in you?

Gaining this clarity is the crucial first step on the challenging but worthwhile journey of rebuilding trust and saving your marriage. In the following chapters, we'll dive deeper into the steps and strategies to make that possible. Stay with me. You've already taken the brave first step by seeking guidance.

Chapter Two

The Many Faces of Trust

I n ancient Hebrew, the main word for 'trust' also means a place of refuge that you flee to for protection. Other terms, which translate as 'trust,' contain the elements of being secure, confident, and hopeful. When referring to 'false trust,' the term refers to writhing in pain, conveying the experience in vivid terms. With this definition, 'trusting' someone means that you take refuge and seek safety in what they tell you. You are placing hope in what they are telling you.

Imagine a couple, Michelle and Dave, who have been married for ten years. Michelle has always trusted Dave implicitly, viewing him as her rock and safe haven. However, when she discovers that Dave has been having an affair, that trust is shattered. Suddenly, Michelle no longer feels secure or hopeful in their relationship. The very foundation of their marriage has been shaken, and Michelle is left feeling vulnerable and betrayed. She wonders if she can trust him to protect her since he has been unable to protect their marriage.

The Greek word translated as 'trust' is in the active sense. Being active, the word conveys the idea that trust acts on those involved. It initiates activity. It engages in binding people together, persuading them, and placing confidence in them. According to the Greek definition, trust fundamentally changes relationships: the more trust, the tighter the bond between two people.

In the aftermath of Dave's affair, Michelle struggles to trust him again. The bond that once held them together has been severely damaged, and Michelle finds it difficult to have confidence in Dave's words and actions. Rebuilding that trust will require both partners' active effort as they persuade each other of their commitment and loyalty.

Even the word 'confidence', used in defining trust, is a compound word made up of 'con' and 'fidence'. The root word 'con' returns to its Latin roots, meaning 'with'. 'Fidence' also stems from a Latin root, 'fides' or fidelity, carrying with it the concepts of loyalty and being true to a person or cause. So when you place 'confidence' in someone, you are giving them your loyalty while at the same time counting on them being loyal to you as well. It is within a common bond of loyalty that confidence is given.

'Trust' is also a term used in law and real estate. Although there is some overlap, there are differences in how the term is used. You may not be concerned with real estate or legal trusts, but these definitions will help you understand the many uses of 'trust.'

In its legal application, 'trust' is a relationship where you can use property within a specified range of acceptable limits. You are expected to do what is best for the property in question. The trusted person is expected to do what is 'in the best interest' of the property in question. This is kind of like booking a hotel reservation for the weekend. You are expected to show up. You are also expected to treat the room and its contents in a reasonable manner.

On the other hand, in real estate, 'trust' is a relationship where the trustee (the person in whom the trust is placed) is responsible for managing or handling a property or funds. In handling that property, it is expected that the trustee is operating in the best interest of the person placing the trust in them. This is more like having a travel agent arrange your weekend for you – or, of course, trusting a real estate agent to handle your home purchase.

In the context of infidelity, trust can be likened to the legal and real estate definitions. When you trust your partner, you essentially give them the freedom to interact with others within acceptable boundaries, expecting them to do what is best for your relationship. An affair is a breach of that trust, much like a tenant damaging a hotel room or a trustee mismanaging funds.

As you can see, the simple word 'trust' has many applications. When you are using the term, it helps to be clear on what you mean and to find out what your spouse means when they use it. When you and your spouse infer different meanings from those intended, the discussion you think you are having about trust may be far different from what your spouse is hearing. Since the mind can play tricks on you or may even be helping the cheater to twist and distort matters, being clear and specific about the terms you are using and what you mean is important.

For example, saying, "I can't trust you anymore!" could have several applications. It is unclear if you are talking about trusting their parenting, handling financial matters, social skills, drinking, or the ability to keep secrets. Without any clarification, when allowed to choose their definition of what you mean, they will often choose one you did not intend.

Consider this scenario: After discovering Dave's affair, Michelle tells him, "I can't trust you anymore!" Dave, feeling defensive, responds, "What do you mean? I'm a great father, and I've always been responsible with our finances." In this case, Dave is choosing to interpret Michelle's statement in a way that minimizes his betrayal and shifts the focus away from the affair. Michelle must be specific about what aspect of trust has been broken and what she needs from Dave to rebuild that trust.

Rebuilding trust after an affair requires both partners to be open, honest, and specific in their communication. The betrayed partner must be clear about their feelings and what they need to feel safe and secure in the relationship again. The partner who had the affair must be willing to take responsibility for their actions, be transparent, and consistently demonstrate their commitment to the relationship through their words and actions.

Some practical steps for couples working to rebuild trust include:

1. Setting clear boundaries and expectations for behavior and communication

2. Regularly checking in with each other about feelings and progress

3. Attending individual and/or couples therapy to work through underlying issues and improve communication skills

4. Practicing vulnerability and emotional intimacy through open, honest conversations

5. Making time for shared activities and experiences to rebuild positive connections

Rebuilding trust is a gradual process that requires patience, commitment, and a willingness to confront difficult emotions and conversations. It's not easy, but it is possible for couples to emerge from the devastation of an affair with a stronger, more resilient bond.

Trust Exercise:

Take a moment to reflect on the following questions:

1. When you say, "I can't trust you anymore," what specific aspects of trust have been broken in your relationship?

2. What do you need from your partner to start feeling safe and secure in the relationship again?

3. How can you clearly and specifically communicate your needs and expectations around trust?

4. What steps can you and your partner take today to rebuild trust and strengthen your bond?

By exploring these questions and discussing them openly with your partner, you can begin the process of healing and restoring trust in your relationship.

In the next chapter, we'll explore the emotional impact of broken trust and strategies for coping with the pain and uncertainty that often follow an affair.

Chapter Three

The Leap of Faith

When addressing the topic of trust, the therapist Erik Erikson used the metaphor of taking a leap to illustrate the nature of trust. The metaphor of a *"leap of faith"* is similar. When a person takes such a leap, they trust their ability to land safely at their destination. The person places hope in their leap and confidence in the safety of their landing.

In psychology circles, an exercise called a 'trust fall' is used. The exercise involves one person, the "faller," deliberately falling backward, trusting that another person, the "catcher," will be there to catch them and prevent them from hitting the ground.

Similarly, couples trust their partner to be there for them. They also hope their partner views them as trustworthy and trusts them. This mutual trust provides a foundation for a couple to take 'leaps' of forward motion in the progression of their relationship.

Consider the story of Emily and Michael, a couple who had been married for 12 years when Michael discovered that Emily had been having an affair with a coworker. The revelation shattered the trust that had been the bedrock of their relationship. Suddenly, the future felt unstable and uncertain.

For Emily and Michael, the aftermath of the affair was a time of intense emotional turmoil. Emily struggled with guilt and shame over her actions, while Michael grappled with feelings of betrayal, anger, jealousy, and profound sadness. They both felt stuck, unable to move forward because the trust that had once been so strong between them had been badly damaged.

This is part of the reason that you may feel stuck or motionless when you are faced with a trust crisis that occurs with an affair. Your leaps become scary and uncertain when the trust is gone or damaged. Any future momentum is now unsure because there is a loss of hope, a loss of a sense of safety, and a loss of certainty.

The impact of broken trust can be far-reaching, affecting not just the emotional connection between partners but also their sense of self and ability to function in the relationship. When trust is shattered, it's common for the betrayed partner to question their own judgment, wondering how they could have missed the signs or been so easily deceived. They may struggle with self-doubt, wondering if they can ever trust their own perceptions again. So there is damage to the relationship between the couple and between the betrayed and their own judgment and confidence.

For the partner who had the affair, the loss of trust can be equally devastating. They may feel profound guilt and shame over their actions and struggle to forgive themselves. They may also feel a sense of hopelessness, wondering if they will ever be able to regain their partner's trust and rebuild the relationship they have damaged.

It is not by accident that Erikson also views trust as the foundational element of human development. Like the foundation of a home, all future social growth and progress depends on a solid foundation of "trust." Trust needs to be established to some extent before people can progress in their development; Erikson viewed trust and its formation as essential for all future development. Once trust is formed, fidelity can evolve. Erikson defined fidelity as the ability to trust, taken to a higher level. Erikson saw a clear connection between trust and fidelity.

This connection between trust and fidelity is particularly salient in the context of infidelity. When one partner chooses to have an affair, they are not only breaking their partner's trust but also shattering the fidelity that is the very basis of the relationship. This betrayal can feel like an existential threat to the relationship, questioning everything the couple has built together.

Rebuilding trust after an affair is a difficult and painful process, but it is possible. It requires both partners' willingness to confront the difficult emotions and challenges that arise and to work together to create a new foundation of trust and fidelity.

For Emily and Michael, this process began with honest, open communication. Emily had to be willing to take responsibility for her actions, thoughts, and emotions. She also had to answer Michael's questions about the affair with complete transparency, no matter how challenging the questions were. Michael, in turn, had to be willing to listen and try to understand what had led Emily to make the choices she did. He obviously did not agree with her choices but was willing to hear her out.

They also had to work to establish new boundaries and expectations for their relationship moving forward. This meant having difficult conversations about what fidelity and commitment meant to each of them and what specific behaviors and actions they needed from each other to feel safe and secure in the relationship again.

Seeking the guidance of a qualified therapist was also an important step for Emily and Michael. It was invaluable to have a neutral third party to help them navigate the complex emotions and challenges of rebuilding trust. Their therapist provided them with tools and strategies for communication, conflict resolution, and emotional regulation to practice together. They had to learn not to interrupt each other and avoid name-calling.

Over time, through consistent effort and a willingness to be vulnerable with each other, Emily and Michael began to see progress. They started to feel more connected and secure in their relationship and were able to start making plans for the future again. They knew rebuilding trust would be ongoing, but they were committed to working together.

Since trust is so foundational, when it is damaged, one feels like they are going back to the start of their relationship. Those struggling with trust often describe it as feeling like they have taken some steps backward or are "back at square one."

Even though it may feel like you are starting over, you are not back at square one. You benefit from all the experiences and growth you have shared as a couple up until now. You are not the same people you were when you first met, and your relationship is not the same either.

Instead of viewing this as starting over, try to see it as an opportunity to build something new and stronger together. You can create a relationship based on a deeper level of honesty, vulnerability, and commitment than ever before.

As you work to rebuild trust, take some time to reflect on the following questions:

1. What does trust mean to you in the context of your relationship?

2. How has the affair impacted your ability to trust your partner? What specific behaviors or actions would help you start to rebuild that trust?

3. What do you need from your partner to feel safe and secure in the relationship again? How can you communicate those needs clearly and openly?

4. What small steps can you take together to start rebuilding intimacy and connection in your relationship?

Rebuilding trust takes time, effort, and a willingness to be vulnerable with each other. But if you are both committed to the work, you can emerge from this challenge with a stronger, more resilient, and more ful-filling relationship than ever before.

TRUST EXERCISE

What one thing could your spouse do to help rebuild your trust? Discuss your answer with your partner, and listen openly to their perspective. Remember, rebuilding trust is a collaborative effort that starts with open, honest communication.

Chapter Four

The Ripple Effect of Lost Trust

When trust is shattered by infidelity, the impact reverberates far beyond the relationship between partners. As you begin to navigate the painful aftermath of a partner's affair, you may find yourself grappling with a profound loss of trust that extends to many areas of your life. It's natural to feel as though the very foundation upon which you've built your world has been knocked out from under you, leaving you questioning everything you once believed.

At the center of this crisis is the loss of trust in your partner who cheated. The lies, deceit, and betrayal can leave you feeling you no longer know the person you once loved and relied upon. You may find yourself constantly questioning their words and actions, searching for signs of further deception. This erosion of trust can be particularly acute if your partner was not forthcoming about the affair and you discovered it through other means. The more they hid, the more you will likely find yourself searching.

However, the loss of trust often extends beyond the cheating partner. You may find that your faith in others who were connected to the situation has also been damaged. Perhaps there were friends or family members who knew about the affair but kept it from you or who even actively participated in the deception. The realization that those you once counted on were not honest with you can be a bitter pill to swallow.

Lena, a 38-year-old teacher, experienced this firsthand when she discovered that her husband, Tom, had been cheating on her with a mutual friend. *"It wasn't just the betrayal of my husband that hurt so deeply,"* she shared. *"It was the fact that someone I considered a close friend had been lying to me and helping him cover up the affair. I felt like I couldn't trust anyone anymore."*

The ripple effect of lost trust can touch many aspects of your life, including your relationships with extended family members. If your partner's family knew about the affair or sided with them in the aftermath, you may find it challenging to maintain those connections. The pain of betrayal can be compounded by a sense of being misunderstood or unsupported by those you once considered part of your inner circle.

As you wrestle with these external losses of trust, you may also struggle with a more internal battle - the loss of trust in yourself. It's common for those who have been betrayed to second-guess their own judgment, choices, and intuition. You may find yourself replaying past events, wondering how you could have missed the signs, or doubting your ability to make wise choices in the future.

This self-doubt can be particularly intense if you had suspicions about your partner's infidelity before the truth came to light. Many betrayed partners report having had a gut feeling that something was amiss, but they dismissed those instincts or allowed their partner to explain them away. When the affair is finally revealed, it can be difficult not to blame yourself for not trusting your own intuition.

The loss of self-trust can have far-reaching consequences, impacting many areas of your life. You may struggle to make decisions at work, doubting your ability to handle challenges or lead effectively. Even small, everyday choices can feel overwhelming when you no longer trust your own judgment.

For some, this self-doubt can be paralyzing, leading to a sense of helplessness and inaction. You may find yourself shying away from making any choices at all for fear of making the wrong one. This can lead to a sense of being stuck, unable to move forward, or progress in your healing journey.

If you're experiencing a loss of trust in yourself, it's important to remember that this is a normal and understandable response to the trauma of betrayal. Your world has been turned upside down, and it's natural to question everything you once believed. However, it's crucial not to let this self-doubt consume you or prevent you from taking steps towards healing.

One helpful strategy is to practice self-compassion. Recognize that you are going through an incredibly difficult and painful experience, and treat yourself with the same kindness and understanding you would offer a dear friend in a similar situation. Acknowledge that rebuilding trust - in yourself and others - will take time and effort, and be patient with yourself as you navigate this process. Trust is unlike a light switch you can turn off and on with one simple action.

It can also be beneficial to seek support from a therapist or counselor who specializes in helping individuals and couples heal from infidelity. They can provide tools and strategies for managing self-doubt, rebuilding confidence, and learning to trust your instincts again.

As you work to rebuild trust in the wake of an affair, take time to reflect on your experiences and feelings. Consider the following questions:

TRUST EXERCISE

1. In what specific ways has your partner's infidelity impacted your ability to trust them? What would they need to do to begin rebuilding that trust?

2. Are there other people in your life whose trust you have lost due to the affair? How has this affected your relationships with them?

3. In what ways do you find yourself doubting your own judgment, choices, or intuition? How has this self-doubt impacted your daily life and decision-making?

4. What steps can you take to begin rebuilding trust in yourself? What support or resources might you need to do this?

Healing from infidelity is a journey, and rebuilding trust is a crucial part of that process. Be patient with yourself, seek support when you need it, and trust that with time and effort, you can emerge from this pain with renewed strength, wisdom, and confidence in yourself and your path forward.

Chapter Five

The Shattered Landscape of Trust

Sophie stared at the text message on her husband's phone, her heart pounding in her chest. It was from a woman she didn't know, and the words were intimate and flirtatious. At that moment, Sophie felt her world shatter into a million pieces. The trust she had placed in her husband, Ethan, the man she had built a life with for over a decade, crumbled like a house of cards.

As Sophie grappled with the revelation of Ethan's affair, she realized that the damage extended far beyond their marriage. She questioned every aspect of her life, from her relationships with friends and family to her own judgment and intuition. The betrayal had sent shock waves through every corner of Sophie's existence, leaving her feeling lost and alone in a landscape where trust had been obliterated.

As Sophie struggled with the betrayal, she realized the damage extended far beyond her marriage. She pulled away from friends and family, unsure who she could trust. Even those who had been supportive felt somehow tainted by association with Ethan and the affair. Once warm and close, Sophie's relationships with her in-laws became strained and distant.

The impact of infidelity on trust can be insidious, touching even the most peripheral relationships and interactions. You may find yourself questioning the motives of coworkers, neighbors, or acquaintances, wondering if they knew about the affair or played some role in facilitating it. This erosion of trust can leave you feeling isolated and alone, uncertain who you can rely on for support. At times there may even be suspicions bordering on paranoid qualities.

It's important to remember that the loss of trust you're experiencing is a normal and understandable response to the trauma of betrayal. Your distrust does not reflect your character or signify weakness. It's a natural self-protective mechanism, an attempt by your psyche to shield you from further harm. If you have a history of being traumatized, it may take longer to recover. At times, there may be bleed-over from those early life traumas.

However, this distrust can sometimes extend to the support systems and resources you need most in the aftermath of an affair. You may be skeptical of therapists, support groups, or legal professionals, wondering if they truly have your best interests at heart. This hesitancy is valid and understandable, but it's crucial not to let it prevent you from seeking the help and guidance you need.

Sophie struggled with this as well, initially resisting the idea of couples counseling or individual therapy. She feared that opening up to a stranger would make her vulnerable to further betrayal or manipulation. She did not want to be betrayed again. It was only after a close friend shared her own positive experience with therapy that Sophie began to consider it as an option.

If you're struggling to trust the support systems available to you, remember that rebuilding trust is a gradual process. It's okay to start small, perhaps by confiding in a trusted friend or family member before engaging with professionals. As you begin to have positive experiences and interactions, you may find your ability to trust slowly expanding.

It's also important to be gentle with yourself as you navigate this new shattered landscape. Recognize that your distrust is not a personal failing but rather a reflection of the deep wound you've suffered. Allow yourself to set boundaries and communicate your needs clearly, even if that means stepping back from certain relationships or situations.

As you work to rebuild trust in the wake of infidelity, consider the following questions:

TRUST EXERCISE

1. In what specific ways has your partner's affair impacted your ability to trust others? Are there certain relationships or situations where you find your distrust particularly acute?

2. How has the loss of trust affected you emotionally? Do you feel more anxious, angry, or withdrawn in your interactions with others?

3. Are there any physical symptoms you've noticed patterns about your distrust, such as difficulty sleeping, changes in appetite, or increased muscle tension?

4. How has your distrust impacted your social life and relationships? Have you found yourself pulling away from certain people or activities?

5. Are there any patterns you've noticed in the types of people or situations you find most challenging to trust? What do these patterns reveal about your own needs and boundaries?

As you navigate this difficult terrain, know that the pain and confusion you're experiencing are valid and real. People and resources are available to support you every step of the way. In the next chapter, we'll explore specific strategies for rebuilding trust and fostering a greater sense of safety and security in your relationships.

Chapter Six

Creating New Trust

Lila sat across from her husband, Evan, her heart still heavy with the weight of his betrayal. It had been months since she discovered his affair, and despite his apologies and promises to change, Lila found herself struggling to trust him again. Whenever he came home late or had to take a phone call in another room, Lila's mind would spiral into a whirlwind of doubts and fears. She longed for the easy, unshakable trust they had once shared, but the path back to that place seemed long and uncertain.

If you're in a similar situation, grappling with the aftermath of infidelity, you may find yourself wondering how to rebuild the trust that was shattered. But as you embark on this journey, shifting your perspective is important. Rather than trying to piece together the broken fragments of your old trust, focus on creating something new – a trust built on a foundation of honesty, transparency, and mutual commitment to healing.

Fear of vulnerability is one of the biggest obstacles to creating new trust. When you've been hurt before, it's natural to want to protect yourself from future pain. You may be holding back and hesitant to fully open up to your partner again. This fear is valid and understandable, but it's important to remember that vulnerability is crucial to intimacy and connection. You face the choice of protecting yourself or getting close to your spouse.

To gradually overcome this fear, start by setting small, achievable goals for vulnerability. This might mean sharing a personal story or expressing a difficult emotion. As you take these small steps and experience positive reactions from your partner, you'll begin to build confidence in your ability to be vulnerable without being hurt.

Another common challenge in creating new trust is the struggle to believe what your partner tells you. After an affair, it's natural to question everything they say, wondering if they're being fully honest. This skepticism is a normal part of the healing process, but it's important not to let it become a roadblock to progress.

One way to work through this is to focus on your partner's actions rather than just their words. Are they transparent with their phone and computer use? Are they following through on their commitments to you and your relationship? Are they willing to have difficult conversations and answer your questions openly and honestly? By paying attention to their behavior, you'll gradually begin to rebuild a sense of trust and reliability. They may even have tells that will alert you to the times when they are dishonest. Look at their eye movements, whether they touch their face or restless body gestures that could indicate lying or deception.

It's also crucial for both partners to be fully engaged in the process of creating new trust. This means the partner who had the affair must be willing to take responsibility for their actions and be patient with the healing process. They need to understand that rebuilding trust takes time and consistent effort, and they can't simply expect their partner to "move on" or "get over it" quickly.

At the same time, the betrayed partner must be willing to gradually let go of the past and focus on the present. This doesn't mean forgetting what happened or excusing the affair, but rather making a conscious choice to work towards a new future together. It means being open to seeing your partner's efforts and progress, even if trust is still a work in progress.

One helpful exercise for couples working to create new trust is the *"trust check-in."* Each day, set aside a few minutes to share one thing that made you feel trusted or respected by your partner and one that may trigger doubts or fears. Use this as an opportunity to have an open, honest conversation about your progress and any areas that need more attention.

Another useful strategy is to work together to establish clear boundaries and expectations for your relationship moving forward. This might include agreements about communication, transparency, and accountability. By creating a shared understanding of what trust looks like in your relationship, you'll have a roadmap to guide you as you move forward.

As you navigate the process of creating new trust, remember to be patient with yourself and your partner. There will be ups and downs, moments of progress and setbacks. But by staying committed to the journey and each other, you can gradually build a stronger, more resilient bond.

In the next chapter, we'll explore the role of forgiveness in the healing process and provide strategies for working through the complex emotions that often arise in the aftermath of an affair. Creating new trust is possible – it just takes time, effort, and a willingness to let go of the past and embrace a new beginning.

Chapter Seven

Trust Before Forgiveness

During a seminar I attended, a fascinating question was asked – *"which comes first: trust or forgiveness?"* It's a question that strikes at the heart of the healing process for many couples dealing with the aftermath of an affair. As Emma and Liam sat in my office, grappling with the fallout of Liam's infidelity, this question hung heavy in the air between them.

Emma looked at me, her eyes filled with a mixture of pain and determination. *"I want to forgive him,"* she said softly, *"but I just don't know how. Every time I try, I'm reminded of what he did, and the hurt feels fresh all over again."*

Liam reached for her hand, but Emma pulled away, not yet ready for his touch. *"I know I messed up,"* Liam said, his voice thick with emotion. *"I'll do whatever it takes to make this right. I just don't know where to start."*

As a therapist who has worked with countless couples in similar situations, I've come to believe that trust must come before forgiveness in the healing process. While both are essential for rebuilding a relationship after an affair, trust is the foundation upon which forgiveness can be built.

Think about it this way: forgiveness is a deeply emotional and spiritual act. It requires a willingness to let go of the hurt and anger, release the pain of the past, and move forward. But how can you forgive someone you don't trust? How can you open your heart to them again when you constantly wonder if they'll betray you again?

That's where trust comes in. By starting with small, concrete acts of trust, you can begin to rebuild the foundation of your relationship. This might mean trusting your partner to follow through on a specific commitment, like coming home at the agreed-upon time or being transparent with their phone and computer use.

As Emma and Liam worked to rebuild trust, they started with these small steps. Liam made a point of always letting Emma know where he was going and who he was with. He gave her access to his phone and email, not because she demanded it, but because he wanted to show her he had nothing to hide.

At first, Emma struggled to extend even this basic level of trust. She constantly checked Liam's phone, looking for signs of betrayal. However, as Liam consistently followed through on his commitments and proved himself transparent and accountable, Emma slowly relaxed her grip.

It's important to recognize that trust after an affair differs from trust before an affair. Pre-affair trust is often blind and unconditional, based on the assumption that your partner would never hurt you. Post-affair trust is more cautious and deliberate, built on a foundation of transparency and accountability.

As you work to rebuild trust, both partners must be fully engaged in the process. The partner who had the affair must be willing to take responsibility for their actions and do the hard work of regaining their partner's trust. This means being patient, understanding, and consistently following through on their commitments.

On the other hand, the betrayed partner must be willing to risk extending trust again. This can be a scary and vulnerable process, especially when the pain of betrayal is still fresh. Sometimes, feeling afraid, uncertain, and even skeptical is normal. But you can gradually rebuild the lost trust by communicating openly and honestly with your partner and taking things one step at a time.

As Emma and Liam continued to work on their relationship, they found that the small acts of trust they had built began to add up to something bigger. Emma no longer needed to constantly check Liam's phone or question his whereabouts. Liam, in turn, felt a renewed commitment to their marriage and a deeper understanding of the impact his actions had on Emma.

They discovered that forgiveness unfolded naturally as they worked to rebuild trust. It wasn't a single moment or decision but rather a gradual softening of the heart and a willingness to let go of the pain of the past.

If you're struggling to rebuild trust after an affair, know that you're not alone. It's a challenging and often painful journey, but it is possible with patience, commitment, and a willingness to take things one step at a time.

TRUST EXERCISE

Take a moment to reflect on five areas where you can extend trust to your partner after an affair. Small, concrete acts or gestures might demonstrate your willingness to take a risk and begin rebuilding your relationship.

1.

2.

3.

4.

5.

Rebuilding trust takes time, effort, and a willingness to be vulnerable. But by starting with these small steps and working together with your partner, you can begin to lay the foundation for a stronger, more resilient relationship.

In the next chapter, we'll explore the role of empathy and understanding in the healing process and offer strategies for cultivating deeper compassion for yourself and your partner as you navigate this challenging journey together.

Chapter Eight

The Misery of Mistrust

Grace sat in her therapist's office, tears streaming down her face as she recounted the painful discovery of her husband's affair. *"I just don't know how to trust him again,"* she whispered, her voice heavy with despair. *"Every time he's late coming home, or I see him texting on his phone, I feel this wave of anxiety and doubt wash over me. It's like I'm constantly waiting for the other shoe to drop, for him to hurt me again."*

Grace's experience is all too common for those who have been betrayed by a partner. The breach of trust that occurs with infidelity shakes the very foundation of a relationship, leaving the betrayed partner feeling lost, hurt, and alone. She feels anxious about the future. But many people don't realize that the pain of mistrust goes far beyond the relationship itself.

As I explored the origins of the word "mistrust," I discovered that it shares the same root as the word "misery." This connection is more than just an interesting linguistic tidbit – it speaks to the profound impact mistrust can have on our overall well-being.

When we mistrust someone, particularly a spouse or partner, we hold onto the painful memories and fears associated with their betrayal. We carry the agony of not knowing what to believe or who to trust. This ongoing misery seeps into every aspect of our lives, affecting our relationship with ourselves, our peace of mind, our distrust regarding the future, and even our physical health.

For Grace, the misery of mistrust manifested in constant anxiety and self-doubt. She found herself questioning her own judgment, wondering how she could have missed the signs of her husband's infidelity. She struggled to find joy in activities that once brought her happiness, feeling weighed down by the burden of her pain.

What made Grace's situation even more challenging was her husband's response to her concerns. Rather than validating her feelings and taking responsibility for what he did, he dismissed or minimized her pain. He would tell her to *"just get over it"* or accuse her of being paranoid and overreacting. But Grace's pain was real. It was not imagining things or overreacting. Her mistrust was a natural response to the betrayal she had experienced. By dismissing her concerns, her husband was only deepening her sense of misery and making it harder for her to heal.

If you're in a similar situation, dealing with the misery of mistrust after a partner's affair, it's important to remember that your feelings are valid. Your pain is real, and you deserve to have your concerns acknowledged and addressed.

One of the most important things a cheating partner can do to help rebuild trust is to validate their partner's feelings. This means listening without judgment, acknowledging the hurt they've caused, and taking responsibility for their actions. It means being patient and understanding, even when the betrayed partner's mistrust feels overwhelming or irrational.

By validating their partner's concerns and sharing in their pain, the cheater creates a safe space for healing to occur. They can show that they are committed to repairing the damage they've caused and rebuilding the trust they've broken.

But rebuilding trust is a two-way street. It requires each person to clean up their side of the street. To the betrayed partner, being honest about your feelings and needs is important. Communicate openly with your partner about what you need from them to feel safe and secure in the relationship again.

TRUST EXERCISE

Take a moment to reflect on how mistrust has impacted your life and relationships. Consider the following questions:

1. What have you lost as a result of mistrust in your relationship?

2. How has your partner's attitude toward your concerns affected you?

3. How has your partner's attitude affected others in your life, such as children or family members?

4. What specific actions or behaviors could your partner engage in to validate your concerns and begin rebuilding trust?

5. How could your partner show empathy and share your pain as you heal?

6. What do you need from your partner to feel safe and secure in the relationship again?

Take your time with these questions, and don't hesitate to journal or discuss your thoughts with a trusted friend or therapist. Your feelings matter, and your pain deserves to be acknowledged and addressed.

Chapter Nine

Understanding Trust

As Sophia sat in her therapist's office, she couldn't help but feel overwhelmed by the question that had been weighing on her mind: *"Will I ever be able to trust him again?"* It had been months since she discovered her husband, Robby, had been having an affair, and the pain still felt raw and all-consuming.

Her therapist, Dr. Kim, leaned forward with a compassionate smile. *"Sophia, I know this is incredibly difficult to wrestle with,"* she said gently. *"But I want you to know that the answer to that question ultimately lies within you. Your ability to trust Robby again will depend on the choices you make and the mindset you cultivate."* Dr. Kim explained a simple but powerful concept: the relationship between choices, mindset, and options. She drew a diagram on a piece of paper:

Choices (will) → Mindset (mental template) → Options (actions)

"You see," Dr. Kim explained, *"the choices we make are a function of our will. They set up our mental programming or mindset. Our mindset, in turn, acts as a mental template that defines the options we perceive as available to us."*

Sophia nodded slowly, taking in this new perspective. She thought about the messages she had been sending herself ever since discovering Robby's affair. *"I'll never be able to trust him again,"* she had told herself repeatedly. *"Once a cheater, always a cheater."*

Dr. Kim seemed to read her thoughts. "The messages we send ourselves have a profound impact on our ability to trust," she said. *"If we constantly tell ourselves that we can't or won't trust our partner again, we create mental and emotional barriers that can prevent trust from growing."*

Sophia sighed heavily. *"But how can I change those messages when the pain feels so overwhelming?"* she asked, her voice trembling.

Dr. Kim reached out and placed a comforting hand on Sophia's arm. *"I know it's not easy,"* she said softly. *"Choosing to trust again after a betrayal is one of the hardest things a person can do. It requires a conscious effort to shift our thinking and emotional responses."*

She went on to explain that rebuilding trust is a gradual process that requires patience, effort, and time. *"Trust grows little by little,"* she said. *It's like a delicate plant that needs careful nurturing and attention."*

Sophia considered this analogy, picturing a tiny seedling pushing its way through the soil. She realized that rebuilding trust would require her to make a choice each day—a choice to water that seedling with positive thoughts and actions, even when her pain and fear felt overwhelming.

However, as she voiced this realization to Dr. Kim, Sophia also acknowledged the importance of Robby's role in the process. *"I know I have the power to choose my own mindset,"* she said, *"but I also need Robby to show me through his actions that he's worthy of my trust again."*

Dr. Kim nodded in agreement. *"You're absolutely right, Sophia. Rebuilding trust is a collaborative effort. While you work on cultivating a more trusting mindset, Robby needs to consistently demonstrate his commitment to your relationship through transparency, honesty, and empathy."*

She encouraged Sophia to have an open and honest conversation with Robby about her needs and expectations as they worked to rebuild trust.

As the session drew to a close, Dr. Kim gave Sophia a gentle smile. "I *know the road ahead may feel daunting,*" she said, "*and I believe in your resilience and capacity to heal. Take things one day at a time, and be patient with yourself and the process.*"

Sophia left the office feeling a glimmer of hope for the first time in months. She knew rebuilding trust would be challenging, but she also recognized the power of her choices and mindset in shaping that journey.

TRUST EXERCISE

Take a moment to reflect on your own internal dialogue about trust and your relationship. Consider the following questions:

1. What messages have you been sending yourself about your partner and your ability to trust them?

2. How might these messages influence your mindset and the options you perceive as available to you?

3. Do you want to trust your partner again? What would it take for you to make that choice?

Your feelings are 100% valid, and the decision to trust again is deeply personal. Be honest with yourself about your needs and boundaries, and don't hesitate to seek support as you navigate this challenging terrain like the young seedling. A path forward is possible with time, effort, and commitment to your own healing.

Chapter Ten

The Shattered Trust of a Child

Renee sat on her bed, hugging her knees tightly to her chest as tears streamed down her face. At just eight years old, her world had been turned upside down by the revelation of her father's affair. She couldn't understand why her daddy, the man she trusted more than anyone else in the world, had chosen to leave their family. The pain of his betrayal cut deeper than she could ever imagine.

When a parent is unfaithful, the damage extends far beyond the marriage itself. The innocent hearts of children, who trust their parents unquestioningly, are left shattered and confused. They rely on their parents for love, security, and guidance; when that sacred bond is broken, the scars last a lifetime.

As Renee struggled to make sense of her new reality, her mother, Carol, felt helpless in the face of her daughter's pain. She knew that the road to healing would be long and difficult for their family, and she worried about the lasting impact the affair would have on Renee's ability to trust others in the future.

It's important to recognize that while children may eventually forgive their parents for the affair, the pain of the betrayal often lingers. They may build emotional walls around their hearts, protecting themselves from the possibility of future hurt. The damage caused by an affair can echo through a child's life long after the initial discovery, affecting their own relationships and sense of security.

As children grow and develop, they may need to revisit the trauma of the affair at different stages. Even if the parents have moved on, children may have new questions or emotions to process as they gain maturity and understanding. Parents must create an open, safe space for their children to express their feelings and work through the impact of the betrayal, no matter how much time has passed.

The pain of an affair is compounded when it involves not just a parent but other family members as well. Grandparents, aunts, uncles, and cousins who may have known about the infidelity or taken sides can leave children feeling even more lost and alone. The people they once looked to for love and support may now feel like sources of confusion and distrust.

If you find yourself navigating the aftermath of an affair with your children, remember that honesty and empathy are essential. You also have to allow them to heal at their own pace. While it may be tempting to shield them from the truth to protect them, children are often more perceptive than we give them credit for. They sense when something is wrong, and hiding the reality of the situation can ultimately cause more harm than good.

When discussing the affair with your children, tailoring your approach to their age and emotional maturity is important. Younger children may need simpler explanations and more reassurance, while older children may have more complex questions and feelings to work through. Regardless of their age, what matters most is that they feel heard, validated, and loved.

It's also important to recognize that in the wake of an affair, children may struggle to trust both parents, not just the unfaithful one. They may fear that if one parent could betray the family, the other could, too. Rebuilding that trust takes time, patience, and a consistent show of love and commitment from both parents.

For families dealing with the added challenges of special needs children, the impact of an affair can be even more pronounced. The demands and stresses of caring for a child with additional needs can strain even the strongest of marriages, and when infidelity enters the picture, the burden can feel overwhelming. However, it's crucial to remember that these children need and deserve the same love, honesty, and stability as any other child.

If you are a parent who has been betrayed, it's understandable to feel anger and resentment towards your partner. However, keeping those feelings separate from your interactions with your children is important. They need to know that they are not to blame for what happened and that both parents still love them unconditionally.

Healing from the trauma of an affair is a gradual process for the whole family. It requires open communication, emotional vulnerability, and a willingness to work through the pain together. Seeking the support of a therapist or counselor who specializes in working with families can be incredibly beneficial, providing a safe space to process emotions and develop coping strategies.

Your children look to you for guidance and reassurance during this difficult time. By modeling honesty, empathy, and resilience, you can help them navigate the complex emotions they are experiencing and begin the process of rebuilding trust. A big part of their coping is role-modeling healthy ways of dealing with the pain.

Chapter Eleven

How Can I Earn Back My Partner's Trust?

Advice for the Unfaithful Spouse

If you've cheated on your partner, getting them to trust you again may feel insurmountable. And it's true - they have every reason to doubt your trustworthiness right now. In the past, they likely believed whatever you told them simply because you said it. But now that you've shattered the very foundation of your relationship with your infidelity, that blind trust is gone.

It's important to understand that even if your partner forgives you, that doesn't automatically mean they trust you again. Forgiveness and trust are two separate things. If you expect an apology and admission of wrongdoing to be enough to restore their faith in you, you're not being realistic.

Through your cheating, you've demonstrated to your partner that you are not trustworthy. You took the precious gift of their trust and carelessly damaged it, perhaps beyond repair. It's foolish and frankly disrespectful to expect things to return to how they were before. The only way to move forward is to consistently show your partner through your actions that you are making real changes and doing the work to become worthy of their trust again.

One or two isolated acts of trustworthiness aren't going to cut it. Your betrayed partner is going to test you over and over again. This is a natural response to the trauma of infidelity. They need to see if you can be relied upon to tell the truth, keep your word, and put their needs above your selfish desires. How you respond to these tests, both in your words and demeanor, will play a huge role in determining whether trust can be rebuilt.

If you get defensive, dismissive, or impatient with your partner's ongoing need for reassurance and proof of your commitment, you show them that you're still primarily focused on yourself and your comfort. But if you can meet each test with empathy, accountability, and a steadfast dedication to doing whatever it takes to heal the damage you've caused, you'll be laying the foundation for a new kind of trust to slowly take root.

Earning back trust after an affair is a long, difficult journey with no guarantees. The process will likely be painful and humbling for you. You'll have to be radically honest about the selfish choices and character flaws that led you to betray your partner. You'll have to develop genuine remorse, not just guilt over getting caught. You'll have to learn to put your partner's feelings and needs at the center of your decisions and priorities.

Most of all, you'll have to develop the integrity to do the right thing even when no one is watching, simply because it's the right thing to do. Trust is built on a foundation of consistent, reliable behavior over time. It requires making the choice each day to be the kind of person your partner can believe in and feel safe with again.

If you're serious about restoring trust, look honestly at your past actions. What specific behaviors damaged your credibility with your partner? Was it the sexual betrayal itself? The lies you told to conceal the truth? Broken promises about ending the affair? Identify the concrete ways you've given your partner reason to doubt you.

Then, ask your partner what they need to see from you to rebuild trust. Do they need full transparency, with access to your phone, email, and social media? A commitment to individual counseling to work on your issues? More frequent check-ins when you're apart? Proactively tell them what steps you're willing to take, for as long as it takes, to re-establish their belief in your faithfulness and trustworthiness.

Understand that they may need more accountability and reassurance from you than feel comfortable. That's understandable, given the magnitude of your betrayal. If you truly want to save your relationship, you'll be willing to do whatever it takes, for however long it takes, to help your partner feel safe again. There is no quick fix or easy shortcut. Trust can only be rebuilt through the slow, steady work of showing up as your best self, day in and day out.

The road ahead won't be easy. However, trust can be rebuilt over time if you and your partner are fully committed to healing. By taking full responsibility for your actions, developing deep empathy for your partner's pain, and consistently following through on your promises, you can slowly show them that you are worthy of their trust again.

TRUST EXERCISES

1. List how you lied, deceived, and betrayed your partner. Write down how you imagine each of those actions made them feel. Read this list daily as a reminder of the damage caused by your choices.

2. Have an honest conversation with your partner about what they need from you to regain their trust. Listen with an open heart, without

defensiveness. Commit to following through on their requests, even when it's hard.

3. Develop a daily practice of self-reflection. Journal about your progress, setbacks, and ongoing commitment to being a trustworthy partner. Share these reflections with your partner if they're open to it.

With dedication, accountability, and the humility to keep showing up even when you stumble, it is possible to overcome infidelity and build a stronger relationship than ever before. Trust can bloom again in even the rockiest soil—as long as you're willing to tend to it with great care, one day at a time.

Chapter Twelve

The 111-Minute Expectation

Why Rebuilding Trust Takes Time

In today's fast-paced world, we've grown accustomed to instant grati-fication. We want everything to happen quickly and neatly, just like in the movies. When it comes to healing a marriage after an affair, many couples fall into the trap of expecting their issues to be resolved within the span of a Hollywood film - typically around 111 minutes. This unrealistic expectation can seep into our minds, making us believe that even the most complex, painful problems can be fixed in a matter of hours.

Take Tammy and Mark, for example. When Tammy discovered that Mark had been unfaithful, she was devastated. The trust that had been the bedrock of their marriage was shattered in an instant. In the aftermath of the revelation, they both desperately wanted to find a way to move forward, to heal the deep wounds caused by the affair. They hoped that a few intense conversations or a handful of therapy sessions would be enough to put the pieces of their relationship back together.

But as they soon discovered, rebuilding trust after an affair is not quick or easy. It cannot be rushed or forced into a predetermined timeline. Expecting to resolve such a profound betrayal in a single conversation or even a few weeks of counseling is unrealistic - it can add unnecessary pressure to an already challenging situation.

Think about it this way: 100 minutes into a serious discussion about infidelity, most couples are still barely scratching the surface of all the complex emotions, unmet needs, and broken agreements that led to the affair in the first place. Trying to cram all that pain, fear, and disappointment into a short window is a recipe for frustration and disillusionment.

Couples who approach their healing journey without the pressure of a rigid timeline often make more meaningful progress than those who try to rush the process. By permitting themselves to take things one day at a time, to sit with the discomfort and uncertainty, they create space for genuine growth and reconnection.

Another common pitfall is the belief that all the issues surrounding the affair can be addressed in a single conversation or therapy session. Some couples, desperate to put the pain behind them, try to deal with the infidelity "once and for all." They want to say everything that needs to be said to make all the necessary changes in one fell swoop. But this approach often backfires, creating even more problems than it solves.

When we try to cram all our hurt, anger, and insecurity into a single conversation, we pressure ourselves and our partner to get it "right" the first time. But healing from an affair is not a once-and-done event - it's an ongoing process that requires patience, perseverance, and a willingness to have difficult conversations over and over again until trust is slowly rebuilt.

On the other end of the spectrum, some couples fall into the trap of believing that things will never change and that the damage caused by the affair is irreparable. They might say things like, "I'll never be able to trust them again," or "Our marriage will never be the same." While these feelings are completely understandable after such a profound betrayal, they can become a self-fulfilling prophecy if we're not careful.

The truth is that change after an affair may be slow and incremental, but that doesn't mean it's not happening. Small moments of vulnerability, accountability, and reconnection can easily be missed or minimized if we're stuck in an "all or nothing" mindset. By learning to celebrate even the tiniest steps forward, we keep the flame of hope alive and create momentum toward lasting, meaningful change.

So, how long does it take to rebuild trust after infidelity? The honest answer is, it depends. Every couple's journey is unique, shaped by their circumstances, personalities, and commitment to doing the hard work of healing. Some may feel a renewed sense of connection and security within a few months, while others may need a year or more to feel like they're back on solid ground.

The key is approaching the process with realistic expectations and an open heart. Rather than fixating on a specific timeline or endpoint, focus on showing up for yourself and your partner each day with patience, empathy, and a willingness to sit with the discomfort. Trust is rebuilt in the small moments - a heartfelt apology, a gentle touch, a kept promise. By stringing those moments together, one day at a time, you gradually weave a new foundation of trust and intimacy.

If you're struggling to let go of the 111-minute expectation, try this simple exercise:

1. Sit down with your partner, and each of you write down your best guess for how long it will take you to feel a sense of trust and security in your relationship again.

2. Share your answers without judgment or criticism. Notice any differences or similarities in your expectations.

3. Have an honest conversation about rebuilding trust for each of you. What specific actions, behaviors, or milestones would help you feel like you're making progress?

4. Commit to checking in with each other regularly about your healing process. Celebrate the small victories and offer each other grace and understanding when setbacks occur.

There is no magic formula or perfect timeline to rebuild broken trust. What matters most is that you're both committed to showing up, doing the hard work, and believing in the possibility of a stronger, more authentic connection on the other side.

Chapter Thirteen

To Spy or Not to Spy

Navigating Trust in the Aftermath of an Affair

When suspicions of infidelity arise, many betrayed partners find themselves grappling with a difficult question: should I spy on my spouse to uncover the truth? While the desire for answers is understandable, spying can be risky, sending a clear message about the lack of trust in the relationship.

Consider the story of Amanda and Chris. When Amanda begins to suspect that Chris is cheating, she is consumed by the need to know the truth about 'everything.' She starts checking his phone when he isn't looking, driving by his office to see if his car is there, and even hiring a private investigator to follow him. When Chris eventually discovers her spying, he is furious.

"Don't you trust me?" he demanded, his voice filled with a mixture of anger and incredulity. Amanda was taken aback by his response. After all, wasn't he the one who violated their marriage vows? Wasn't she justified in her suspicions?

However, as Amanda soon realized, the issue of trust in the wake of an affair is rarely straightforward. Cheaters often react strongly to any perceived lack of trust, even when their actions have clearly undermined the very foundation of the relationship. They may try to flip the script, painting the betrayed partner as the one with the problem for not blindly believing in their innocence.

This kind of gaslighting can leave the betrayed partner feeling confused, guilty, and even crazy. They may question their own perceptions and intuition, wondering if they're overreacting or imagining things. If they approach the issue of spying from a place of outright distrust, they may find themselves on the defensive, struggling to justify their actions in the face of their partner's righteous indignation.

But what if there was another way to approach the conversation? Instead of focusing solely on the lack of trust, the betrayed partner could frame their decision to spy regarding the growing distance and disconnection in the relationship. They might say something like, "I've been feeling so alone and afraid of losing you lately. I know spying wasn't the right way to handle my fears, but I didn't know what else to do. I want us to find a way to be close again."

By shifting the emphasis from the cheater's past actions to the future of the relationship, the betrayed partner may be able to diffuse some of the defensiveness and create an opening for more honest dialogue. This approach acknowledges the betrayed partner's own role in the situation without absolving the cheater of responsibility for their choices.

Of course, this is easier said than done. When faced with evidence of a partner's infidelity, it's natural to want to confront them with cold, hard facts and demand accountability. The temptation to gather as much proof as possible can be overwhelming, leading to increasingly invasive forms of spying.

But it's important to remember that there's no going back once the truth emerges. The knowledge of a partner's betrayal can never be erased, and the pain and mistrust it engenders can linger long after the affair ends. Before you engage in spying, it's worth asking yourself what you hope to achieve and what you'll do with the information once you have it.

Will knowing every detail of your partner's transgression help you heal and move forward, or will it only deepen your pain and resentment? Are you prepared to leave the relationship if your worst fears are confirmed, or are you committed to working through the betrayal together?

There are no easy answers, but it's important to approach the decision to spy with a clear head and an open heart. If you decide to gather evidence, be prepared for your partner to feel violated and betrayed by your actions, even if you feel justified in taking them. Trust is a two-way street; rebuilding it will require both partners to be honest, vulnerable, and accountable.

Ultimately, deciding to spy or not to spy is a deeply personal one that each couple must navigate based on their unique circumstances. But regardless of how you choose to uncover the truth, the real work of healing and rebuilding trust can only begin once all the secrets are laid bare.

If you find yourself grappling with the issue of spying in your own relationship, consider the following exercise:

1. Take some time to reflect on your motivations for wanting to spy on your partner. Are you seeking clarity, control, or revenge? What do you hope to gain from knowing the truth?

2. Talk honestly with your partner about your fears and concerns. Use "I" statements to express how their actions have made you feel rather than attacking or blaming them for your decision to spy.

3. Set clear boundaries and expectations for transparency and accountability moving forward. If your partner is committed to rebuilding trust, they should be willing to take concrete steps to prove their trustworthiness, such as sharing passwords or agreeing to regular check-ins.

4. Seek support from a trusted friend, family member, or therapist as you navigate this difficult time. Remember that you don't have to face this challenge alone.

At the end of the day, rebuilding trust after an affair is a long and difficult journey that requires patience, perseverance, and a willingness to confront painful truths. By approaching the issue of spying with honesty, empathy, and a focus on the future, you can create a foundation for healing and growth, one day at a time.

Chapter Fourteen

Rebuilding Trust

The Power of Communication, Honesty, Commitment, and Time

In the aftermath of an affair, one of the most daunting challenges couples face is rebuilding the shattered trust that once formed the foundation of their relationship. While there is no magic formula or quick fix for repairing the damage caused by infidelity, there is a powerful framework that can guide couples on their journey toward healing and reconnection.

The formula for understanding and rebuilding trust can be summed up in this simple equation:

Trust = Communication + Honesty + Commitment + Time

Let's take a closer look at each component of this equation and how it contributes to restoring trust.

Communication: The Lifeblood of Trust

Open, honest communication is at the heart of any strong relationship. When trust has been broken by an affair, it's more important than ever for couples to create a safe, accepting space where they can share their thoughts, feelings, and needs without fear of judgment or retaliation.

Consider the story of Yvonne and Wesley. When Yvonne discovered that Wesley had been unfaithful, her first instinct was to shut down and withdraw from him emotionally. She couldn't bear the thought of talking about the pain and betrayal she was feeling, so she retreated into silence.

But as the days turned into weeks, Yvonne realized that her silence deepened their chasm. She knew that if they had any hope of rebuilding their relationship, they would need to start communicating openly and honestly with each other.

When Yvonne finally found the courage to share her hurt and anger with Wesley, she was surprised by his response. Instead of getting defensive or dismissive, he listened intently, acknowledging the pain he had caused and expressing his deep remorse. Yvonne felt heard and validated for the first time in a long time.

As Yvonne and Wesley continued to engage in regular, heartfelt conversations, they began to rediscover the emotional intimacy that had been lost in the wake of the affair. They learned to express their needs and boundaries clearly without resorting to threats, put-downs, or sarcastic remarks that could erode the fragile trust they were working so hard to rebuild.

Honesty: The Foundation of Trust

The principle of honesty is closely intertwined with communication. Your relationship may be filled with communication, but it is of limited use if your partner cannot believe what you are telling them.

For trust to flourish, both partners must be willing to be forthright and transparent in their interactions. This means telling the truth and following through on promises and commitments.

For Wesley, honesty meant coming clean about the full extent of his affair, even when it was painful or embarrassing to admit. It meant being accountable for his actions and taking concrete steps to prove his trustworthiness, such as sharing his phone and email passwords with Yvonne and checking in regularly when he was apart from her.

At times, the truth was hard for Yvonne to hear. She didn't always like what Wesley had to say, but she learned to honor his honesty and vulnerability, knowing that it was an essential part of their healing process.

Commitment: The Glue That Holds Trust Together

Rebuilding trust after an affair requires both partners' deep, unwavering commitment to preserve and grow their relationship. It means showing up day after day, even when the work is hard and the progress feels slow. It amounts to staying 'in relationship' with each other, even when you are angry with each other.

For Yvonne and Wesley, commitment meant prioritizing their marriage, even when life's other demands threatened to pull them in different directions. It meant being patient and persistent, even when they were tempted to give up or revert back to old patterns of behavior.

Most importantly, commitment meant choosing each other and their relationship over and over again. It meant believing in the possibility of a stronger, more authentic connection on the other side of the betrayal and being willing to do whatever it took to get there.

Time: The Great Healer of Trust

Finally, rebuilding trust after an affair requires perhaps the most precious commodity of all: time. There is no set timeline for healing from infidelity, no magic number of days or weeks or months that will erase the pain and restore the bond that was broken.

For some couples, rebuilding trust may take six months to a year or more. For others, it may be a lifelong journey of growth and re-commitment. The key is approaching the process with patience, compassion, and a willingness to take things one day at a time.

As Yvonne and Wesley discovered, rebuilding trust is not a linear process. There were days when they felt closer than ever and others when the pain of the betrayal felt as fresh as the day it happened. But as they continued to communicate honestly, act with integrity, and choose each other repeatedly, they slowly began to weave a new fabric of trust and intimacy.

Putting It All Together

Rebuilding trust after an affair is a complex, challenging journey that requires courage, vulnerability, and a deep commitment to growth and healing. By focusing on the four key ingredients of communication, honesty, commitment, and time, couples can slowly but surely create a new foundation of love and trust that is stronger and more resilient than ever before.

If you find yourself struggling to rebuild trust in the aftermath of infidelity, consider the following exercise:

1. Set aside regular, uninterrupted time to have honest, heartfelt conversations with your partner about your feelings, needs, and hopes for the future.

2. List specific actions you and your partner can take to demonstrate your commitment to honesty and transparency in your relationship.

3. Identify one small way to show up for your partner and your relationship each day, even when it feels hard or uncomfortable.

4. Be patient and compassionate with yourself and your partner as you navigate the ups and downs of the healing process. Remember that rebuilding trust takes time and that every small step forward is a victory worth celebrating.

With dedication, perseverance, and a willingness to work on you and your relationship by focusing on trust, it is possible to emerge from the pain of infidelity with a deeper, more authentic connection than ever before. By embracing the power of communication, honesty, commitment, and time, you can slowly but surely rebuild the lost trust and create a love that endures.

Chapter Fifteen

Shining a Light on Secrets

When a spouse's infidelity comes to light, it can feel like stepping into a minefield of secrets and lies. The task of untangling the web of deception and rebuilding trust can seem as daunting as cleaning up a toxic waste spill or removing the rotting carcass of a relationship that has died. It's a messy, unpleasant job that requires equal parts courage, determination, patience, and love.

Consider the story of Laura and Michael. When Laura discovered that Michael had been having an affair with a coworker, she was devastated. But even more painful than the betrayal was the realization that Michael had been keeping secrets from her for months, even years. The lies had become so habitual and ingrained in their daily interactions that Laura hardly knew where to begin sorting out the truth from the fiction.

At first, the prospect of confronting all those secrets head-on felt overwhelming. Laura wanted to bury her head in the sand, to pretend that everything was fine and that the affair had never happened. But deep down, she knew that ignoring the problem would only allow the poison of secrecy to spread, eating away at the very foundation of their marriage.

So Laura took a deep breath and took the first step: she told herself the truth. She acknowledged the pain and betrayal she felt and accepted the reality of what had happened rather than living in denial. It wasn't easy, but it was necessary. Only by being honest with herself could Laura begin to bring truth and transparency back into her relationship with Michael.

As Laura and Michael began the slow, painful process of uncovering and dismantling the secrets between them, they quickly realized that it was not a one-time event but an ongoing journey. The lies and half-truths had become so deeply entrenched in their patterns of communication that it would take time and consistent effort to root them out.

They committed to a few key steps in their quest for honesty:

1. Telling the truth, even when it is uncomfortable or scary

2. Accepting the truth, even when it is painful or disappointing

3. Confronting the lies and secrets as they encountered them with love and firmness

4. Committing to ongoing truth-telling and truth-hearing in their relationship

5. Focusing on the information they truly needed to heal rather than getting lost in unnecessary details

For Laura, this meant being willing to ask difficult questions and hear difficult answers. It meant sitting with the discomfort of not knowing everything and trusting that the truth would emerge in due time. It meant resisting the urge to play detective or interrogator and instead approaching Michael with an open heart and a genuine desire for healing.

For Michael, it meant being willing to be vulnerable and accountable. Instead of avoiding conflicts or unpleasant situations, he had to face and admit the truth. It meant owning up to his mistakes and the damage they had caused without making excuses or shifting blame. It meant being patient and understanding of Laura's need for reassurance and transparency, even when it felt invasive or uncomfortable.

Together, Laura and Michael learned that the power of secrets lies not just in the information they conceal but in the alliances they create. By presenting a united front against the secrets that had divided them, they slowly began to rebuild the trust and intimacy that had been lost.

But the process was not easy, and it required a special kind of love – a tough love willing to confront hard truths and hold each other accountable. Laura and Michael had to learn to speak the truth in love, not in anger or resentment. They had to learn to forgive each other and themselves while still holding firm boundaries around honesty and transparency.

Most importantly, they had to be patient and persistent. Uncovering and releasing the secrets that had accumulated over years of deception was not a task that could be accomplished overnight. It required a daily commitment to truth-telling and truth-seeking, a willingness to confront the lies as they arose, and a deep faith in the power of honesty to heal even the deepest wounds.

As Laura and Michael discovered, shining a light on secrets is not for the faint of heart. It requires courage, vulnerability, and a willingness to step into the mess and discomfort of a relationship in crisis. But by taking that journey together, one step at a time, they slowly cleared away the debris of betrayal and built a new foundation of trust and love.

If you find yourself facing a similar journey of uncovering secrets in the aftermath of infidelity, remember that you are not alone. The path may be challenging, but it leads to healing and wholeness. By committing to accepting the truth, accepting the reality of what has happened, and confronting the lies with love and firmness, you, too, can emerge from the darkness of secrecy into the light of a stronger, more authentic relationship.

Chapter Sixteen

Rebuilding Shattered Trust

When trust is shattered by infidelity, it can feel like the very foundation of your relationship has been ripped away, leaving you lost and disoriented in a pile of rubble. You are not imagining things. The foundation of trust was damaged. You now need a new foundation for trust in your relationship.

But as daunting as it may feel, it's important to remember that trust can be rebuilt, even after the most devastating of betrayals. It's not an easy or quick process, but with time, determination, commitment, and a willingness to do the hard work of healing, couples can emerge from the wreckage of an affair with a stronger, more resilient bond than ever before.

The first step in rebuilding trust is acknowledging the severity of the damage that has been done. An affair is not just a minor indiscretion or a lapse in judgment—it's a fundamental violation of the promises and expectations that form the bedrock of a marriage. When you stand before your beloved on your wedding day and vow to be faithful in good times and bad, you commit to honoring and cherishing your partner above all others. An affair shatters that commitment and the trust that it was built upon.

If you are the partner who has been betrayed, it's important to permit yourself to feel the full range of emotions that come with discovering an affair. The shock, anger, grief, and disbelief can be overwhelming, and it's natural to feel like your world has been turned upside down. You may feel like you no longer know who your partner is or what your relationship stands for.

This is where the hard work of rebuilding begins. As the betrayed partner, you will need to take time to process your emotions and decide whether you are willing to give your partner another chance. This is not a decision to be made lightly or in the heat of the moment. It requires soul-searching, honest communication with your partner and a realistic assessment of whether your relationship is worth fighting for.

If you decide to work towards reconciliation, the first step is establishing a foundation of honesty and transparency. The partner who had the affair must be willing to take full responsibility for their actions and be completely truthful about what happened. This means answering any questions the betrayed partner may have, no matter how uncomfortable or painful the answers may be.

It's important to note that some individuals, such as those struggling with addiction or untreated mental health issues, may not be capable of maintaining the level of honesty and commitment required to rebuild trust. In these cases, it may be necessary to put reconciliation on hold until the underlying issues have been addressed through professional treatment and support.

Assuming both partners are willing and able to do the work, the next step is rebuilding trust through small, consistent actions over time. This is where the metaphor of construction comes into play. Just as a destroyed house must be rebuilt brick by brick, trust must be re-established through a series of tiny, everyday gestures of love, respect, and reliability.

This might mean the unfaithful partner checks in more frequently throughout the day, is more open about their whereabouts and activities, and makes a concerted effort to be present and attentive when they are with their spouse. It may mean that when you are with them in public, you look at your spouse rather than be distracted by others. It might mean the betrayed partner is learning to extend small acts of trust and vulnerability, even when it feels scary or counterintuitive.

Most importantly, rebuilding trust requires a deep commitment from both partners to the long-term health and well-being of the relationship. It means showing up day after day, even when it's hard, and prioritizing the relationship over individual desires or impulses. It means being willing to have difficult conversations, confront uncomfortable truths, and do the inner work necessary to create lasting change.

Forgiveness is also an essential component of rebuilding trust. This doesn't mean forgetting what happened or excusing the betrayal, but rather making a conscious choice to release the anger and resentment that can keep you stuck in the past. Forgiveness is a process, not a one-time event, and it requires patience, empathy, and a willingness to let go of the need for retribution or revenge.

Ultimately, rebuilding trust after an affair is a journey of hope and healing. By committing to honesty, transparency, and small acts of love and trust over time, couples can slowly but surely construct a new foundation for their relationship - one that is stronger, more authentic, and more deeply connected than ever.

Most of all, hold onto the hope that a new beginning is possible. With dedication, compassion, determination, and a willingness to do the hard work of healing, you can emerge from the ruins of betrayal and build a love that endures. One brick, one day, one small act of trust at a time, you can reclaim the relationship you once cherished and create a future filled with possibility and promise. It is hard to achieve a victory when you do not believe it is possible.

Chapter Seventeen

"Isn't It Time to Move On?"

The Danger of Dismissing the Pain of Infidelity

In the aftermath of an affair, well-meaning family members and friends may try to encourage the betrayed partner to *"put it behind them"* and move on with their lives. They may say things like, "*It's been months now. Isn't it time to let it go?"* or *"Dwelling on it isn't going to change what happened; you need to focus on the future."*

While these sentiments may come from a place of love and concern, they can do more harm than good. By dismissing or minimizing the pain of infidelity, they inadvertently send the message that the betrayed partner's feelings are not valid or important. They suggest that there should be some arbitrary time limit on grief and healing and that if you haven't *"gotten over it"* by now, there must be something wrong with you.

The truth is, there is no statute of limitations on the hurt and trauma caused by your partner's betrayal. The pain of infidelity can linger for months, years, or even decades after the affair has ended. It can ripple out to affect not just the immediate couple but their children, extended family, and even future generations.

When Kendra found out that her husband Todd had been cheating on her with a coworker, she was devastated. She felt like her entire world had been shattered, and she didn't know how she would ever be able to trust him again. Kendra struggled to understand what had happened in the following weeks and months. She alternated between rage, despair, and a numbness that felt like it would never end.

Kendra's mother, trying to be supportive, often said things like, *"I know it hurts now, but it's time to put it behind you and focus on your marriage."* But for Kendra, the idea of just moving on felt impossible. How could she forget the lies, the betrayal, the utter disregard for her feelings? How could she pretend everything was fine when her heart was still in a million pieces?

Kendra's mother failed to understand that *"putting it behind you"* is not the same as healing. Trying to rush the healing process or sweep the pain under the rug can prolong the suffering and prevent true recovery.

Affairs are not just a private matter between two consenting adults. They have far-reaching consequences that affect entire families and communities. The betrayal of trust, deceit, and disloyalty are not minor infractions that can be easily brushed aside. They strike at the very heart of what it means to be in a committed, monogamous relationship.

When we try to sidestep the moral implications of cheating or make excuses for the unfaithful partner, we are sending a dangerous message. We are saying that the betrayed partner's pain doesn't matter and that their shattered trust is not a big deal. We are invalidating their experience and their right to grieve the loss of the relationship they thought they had.

Healing from infidelity is not a linear process with a clear endpoint. It is a winding, messy journey that often involves many backward steps and detours. There is no magic formula or timeline for when the pain will subside, and trust will be restored. Every person and every relationship is different.

What betrayed partners need most in the aftermath of an affair is not platitudes or pressure to move on but empathy, validation, and support. They need to know that their feelings matter and that they have the right to take as much time as they need to process what has happened. They need a safe space to express their anger, sadness, and fear without judgment or dismissal.

At the same time, it's important to recognize that healing is possible, even after the most devastating of betrayals. With time, patience, and a willingness to do the hard work of recovery, couples can emerge from the wreckage of an affair stronger and more connected than ever before.

This is where the role of a skilled therapist or counselor can be invaluable. A trained professional can help couples navigate the complex emotions and challenges that come with rebuilding trust and intimacy after infidelity. They can provide tools and strategies for communication, conflict resolution, and reconnection.

Perhaps most importantly, a therapist can offer a nonjudgmental, objective perspective that can be hard to find from family and friends. They can help the betrayed partner validate their feelings and set healthy boundaries while supporting the unfaithful partner in taking responsibility for their actions and making amends.

Ultimately, the journey of healing from infidelity is a deeply personal one. There is no one-size-fits-all approach or timeline. What matters most is that betrayed partners feel seen, heard, and supported as they navigate this difficult terrain.

So the next time someone tells you it's time to *"put it behind you"* and move on, remember this: Your pain is valid. Your healing journey is your own. And you have the right to take all the time and space you need to grieve, rage, and rebuild - without anyone else telling you how to feel or how long it should take.

Chapter Eighteen

The Trustworthiness of an Adulterer

Why Character Matters

It's easy to become jaded about the personal lives of public figures and leaders. When a celebrity or politician is caught in an extramarital affair, the news cycle explodes with salacious details and speculation, only to quickly move on to the next big story. But while society may be tempted to dismiss adultery as a private matter or a mere lapse in judgment, the truth is that infidelity raises serious questions about an individual's overall trustworthiness and character.

Consider the story of Brenda, a successful CEO who had an affair with her married colleague, Tim. Brenda's professional reputation took a major hit when the affair was eventually exposed. Her employees, clients, and board members began questioning her integrity and judgment, wondering if someone who could so easily betray her spouse could be trusted to lead a company with honesty and transparency.

At its core, adultery is an act of deception and disloyalty. When an individual chooses to step outside the bounds of their marriage vows, they betray their spouse's trust and demonstrate a willingness to lie and deceive to serve their interests. They may call it love or passion. This fundamental lack of integrity should give us pause when considering whether to trust an adulterer in other areas of life.

Think about it this way: if someone is capable of lying to the person they have promised to love and cherish above all others, what would stop them from lying to their constituents, their colleagues, or their friends? If they are willing to disregard the sacred vows they made before God and/or the law, how can we trust them to uphold the duties and responsibilities of their public office or professional position?

Some may argue that personal and professional lives should be kept separate and that an individual's behavior in their marriage has no bearing on their ability to lead or serve in other capacities. But the reality is that our personal choices and values are deeply intertwined with our public personas and actions. A leader who lacks integrity and trustworthiness in their private life is unlikely to suddenly develop those qualities in their professional sphere.

Moreover, the ripple effects of adultery extend far beyond the individuals directly involved. When a public figure or leader is caught in an affair, it can have devastating consequences for their family, their community, and even their entire organization or institution. The betrayal and shame can be felt by spouses, children, and loved ones for years to come, eroding the foundation of trust and stability essential for healthy relationships and societies.

So, what does this mean for us as individuals and as a society? We must be willing to hold our leaders and public figures accountable for their personal integrity and character, not just their professional accomplishments or political ideologies. We must demand honesty, loyalty, and fidelity from those we choose to trust with positions of power and influence.

Of course, this is not to say that individuals who have made mistakes in their personal lives are forever unworthy of trust or redemption. We are all human, and we all have flaws and weaknesses. True trustworthiness is built on a consistent track record of integrity, honesty, and respect for others. It is demonstrated through actions, not just words, and it is earned through the hard work of self-reflection, accountability, and change.

For Brenda and Tim, the road to rebuilding trust and credibility was long and difficult. It required a sincere acknowledgment of the pain and damage they had caused, a commitment to making amends and changing their behavior, and a willingness to be transparent and accountable in all areas of their lives. It also required a deep understanding that their personal choices had far-reaching consequences, not just for themselves but everyone around them.

Remember that character matters as you navigate relationships and decide whom to trust and support. Pay attention to the actions and choices of those in positions of power and influence, not just their words or public personas. Hold yourself and others accountable for the integrity and trustworthiness you expect from your leaders and loved ones.

And if you find yourself on the other side of betrayal, know that healing and forgiveness are possible. With time, patience, and a commitment to doing the hard work of self-reflection and change, even the deepest wounds can begin to mend. The path may be long and difficult, but the destination - a life of integrity, trust, and authentic connection - is worth the journey.

Chapter Nineteen

Navigating Trust After Infidelity

Finding the Right Balance

One of the most challenging questions betrayed partners face in the aftermath of an affair is, *"What kind of trust should I give to the cheater?"* It's a complex issue that requires careful consideration and a deep understanding of the healing process.

When trust has been shattered by infidelity, it's natural to want to protect yourself from further pain and disappointment. You may oscillate between a desperate desire to trust your partner again and an overwhelming fear of being hurt again. This emotional tug-of-war is a normal part of the recovery journey, but it can leave you feeling stuck and unsure of how to move forward.

Many cheaters, eager to put the affair behind them, will press for a quick return to the previous pattern of unquestioning trust. They may plead with you to "just trust me" or insist that you should be able to trust them implicitly, as you did before the affair. But blindly trusting a partner who has recently betrayed you can be a recipe for disaster.

Imagine the story of Amy and Jack. When Amy discovered that Jack had been having an affair with his ex-girlfriend, she was devastated. Jack, desperate to save their marriage, begged Amy to trust him, promising he would never be unfaithful again. Amy, longing to return to the safety and security she had once felt in their relationship, decided to take a leap of faith and trust Jack completely.

But as the weeks went by, Amy found herself growing increasingly anxious and paranoid. Every time Jack came home from work late or had to take a phone call in another room, she was consumed by fear and suspicion. She realized that she had placed her trust in Jack prematurely, without any real evidence that he had truly changed or was committed to rebuilding their relationship.

The truth is that rebuilding trust after an affair is a gradual process that requires patience, consistency, and a willingness to take things one step at a time. Rushing to restore unquestioning trust in a partner who has recently betrayed you is like trying to run a marathon with a broken leg - it's not only unrealistic, but it can also cause further damage and setbacks.

So, what kind of trust should you give to a cheating partner? The answer lies in finding a balance between two different approaches: calculus-based trust and identification-based trust.

Calculus-based trust is a more cautious, measured approach to rebuilding trust after an affair. It involves carefully weighing the costs and benefits of extending trust in specific situations based on your partner's actions and the level of risk involved. It is a trust based on calculations. For example, you might trust your partner to pick up your children from school or handle a joint bank account but not go on an overnight business trip or have unmonitored access to social media.

Calculus-based trust is often necessary for the early stages of affair recovery when emotions are still raw, and the cheating partner has not yet demonstrated a consistent pattern of trustworthiness. It allows you to maintain a sense of safety and security while still moving forward in the healing process.

On the other hand, identification-based trust is a deeper, more organic form of trust that develops over time as both partners work to rebuild their connection and align their values and goals. It involves trusting your partner not just because of what they do but because of who they are and the love you share. This type of trust is based on "who" your spouse is rather than considering costs and benefits.

Identification-based trust is the ultimate goal of affair recovery, but it cannot be rushed or forced. It requires a genuine commitment from both partners to do the hard work of healing, to be patient and understanding with each other, and to consistently choose honesty, transparency, and integrity in all their interactions. You must have 'proof' they are changing before you trust them.

The road to identification-based trust was long and challenging for Amy and Jack. Jack had to take concrete steps to prove his trustworthiness, such as cutting off all contact with his ex-girlfriend, being fully transparent with his phone and email, and actively participating in couples therapy. Amy had to work on healing, set boundaries, communicate her needs, be honest about her hurts, and gradually take small risks to extend trust when it felt safe.

Over time, as they consistently committed themselves to their marriage and each other, Amy and Jack began to experience a deeper, more resilient form of trust. They learned to see each other as husband and wife and true partners and allies. They developed a shared vision for their future and a deep understanding of each other's needs, fears, and dreams.

If you are struggling to navigate the complexities of trust after an affair, remember that there is no one-size-fits-all approach. What works for one couple may not work for another, and what feels right at one stage of the healing process may need to be adjusted as you continue to grow and evolve together.

The key is to be patient, to communicate openly and honestly with your partner, and to focus on rebuilding trust in small, incremental steps. Trusting in incremental steps comes before you can whole-heartedly trust them because they are your spouse. Don't be afraid to seek the guidance of a qualified therapist or counselor who can help you navigate the ups and downs of the recovery process.

Most importantly, remember that rebuilding trust after an affair is not about returning to the way things were before but about creating something new and better together. It's an opportunity to deepen your connection, heal old wounds, and build a stronger, more authentic, and more fulfilling relationship than ever before.

So take a deep breath, be kind to yourself and your partner, and trust in the power of love and forgiveness to guide you through this challenging time. With patience, commitment, and a willingness to do the hard work of healing, you can emerge from the darkness of betrayal into the light of a brighter, more beautiful future together.

Chapter Twenty

Rekindling Romance and Trust After an Affair

When Kathy discovered that her husband, Kevin, had been having an affair with a coworker, she felt like her entire world had shattered. The trust and love that had once been the foundation of their marriage now seemed like a distant memory, replaced by feelings of betrayal, anger, and despair. Kathy wondered if she would ever be able to look at Kevin the same way again, let alone rebuild the intimate, trusting bond they had once shared.

If you have recently survived an affair like Kathy and Kevin, you may be struggling with similar emotions and uncertainties. The pain of infidelity can be all-consuming, leaving you feeling lost, alone, fearful you will be abandoned, and unsure of how to move forward. But while the road to healing may be long and challenging, it is possible to rekindle the love and trust in your relationship - with time, patience, and a commitment to doing the hard work of recovery together.

Acknowledge and Process Your Emotions

One of the first and most important steps in rebuilding your relationship after an affair is to give yourself permission to feel and process the complex emotions that come with betrayal. This may involve:

- Seeking the support of a trained therapist or counselor who specializes in infidelity recovery

- Joining a support group for betrayed partners to connect with others who understand your experience

- Practicing self-care through activities like journaling, meditation, exercise, or creative expression

Having good and bad days is normal in affair recovery. Be patient and compassionate with yourself as you navigate this challenging time.

Have an Open, Honest Conversation

When you feel ready, it's crucial to have an open, honest conversation with your partner about the affair and its impact on yourself and your relationship. This conversation may be difficult and emotionally charged, but it's essential for rebuilding trust and understanding. During this conversation:

- Set aside blame and defensiveness and focus on listening to each other's perspectives

- Take responsibility for your own actions and feelings, and avoid making accusations or generalizations

- Discuss what you both need to feel safe, heard, and supported moving forward

-Be willing to discuss not only what happened but also what you imagined and are fearful of

Kevin, for example, might express his deep remorse for the pain he has caused and his commitment to doing whatever it takes to rebuild trust. Kathy, in turn, might share her fears, doubts, and the specific actions she needs from Kevin to feel secure in the relationship again. She also needs to share how her father walked out on her as a child, and she fears that may happen again.

Make Sacrifices and Step Out of Your Comfort Zone

Rebuilding trust and intimacy after an affair requires both partners to make sacrifices and step outside of their comfort zones. This may look different for each couple, but some examples include:

- The betrayed partner takes a leap of faith and extends trust, even when it feels scary or uncertain. Those fears can be reduced by giving trust incrementally

- The partner who had the affair cutting off all contact with the affair partner and being fully transparent with their phone, email, and whereabouts

Kathy, for instance, might choose to give Kevin another chance, even though some of her still feels wary and afraid. She vacillates between thinking, "Once a cheater, always a cheater," and "believing in second chances." The willingness to try again wins out most of the time.

She starts by trusting him in small increments. Some of those tasks he succeeded at, some he failed at. She did not give up and was willing to work with him rather than control him. Kevin, in turn, shared his phone and email passwords with Kathy, checked in with her more frequently throughout the day, and actively participated in therapy to address the underlying issues that contributed to the affair. Although he sometimes forgot to check in, he changed his habits and made that a priority over time. Kevin had to learn new ways of doing things.

Over time, Kevin discovered the triggers that led to his setbacks. In his case, he was triggered by women from poorer backgrounds whom he could help and take advantage of. Once this was discovered, he and Kathy worked on resisting those temptations and the places where they would happen, along with his desire to be needed.

Prioritize Your Relationship

Above all, rekindling romance and trust after an affair requires both partners' deep, unwavering commitment to prioritize the relationship. This means:

- Showing up for each other consistently, even when it's difficult or uncomfortable
- Being willing to have tough conversations and confront painful truths
- Focusing on creating new, positive experiences and memories together

Kathy and Kevin, for example, might set aside dedicated time each week for date nights, surprise each other with thoughtful gestures, or plan a weekend getaway to reconnect and rekindle their spark. This is a change from each of them doing their own thing and weekends of watching shows on Netflix.

Seek Professional Support

Recovering from an affair is a complex, emotionally challenging process that often benefits from professional guidance. Consider seeking the support of a qualified couples therapist who can help you:

- Navigate the ups and downs of the healing journey. There will be ups and downs. Real life is not like the movies.

- Develop effective communication and conflict-resolution skills. This includes both learning to share from the heart and listening without defensiveness.

-Changing unhealthy habits or patterns that contributed to the affair. This may include changing bedtime routines or increasing check-ins with each other.

- Address individual and relational issues that may have contributed to the affair. The affair is often a cry for help. Consider what is missing or needed in your marriage.

- Rebuild trust, intimacy, and a shared vision for your future together

There is no shame in seeking help. Prioritizing your relationship and investing in professional support can prove your commitment to healing and growth.

Rekindling romance and trust after an affair is a brave, worthwhile journey that requires patience, perseverance, and a willingness to lean into the discomfort and uncertainty of the healing process. You can gradually rebuild a stronger, more resilient bond with your partner by acknowledging your emotions, communicating openly and honestly, making sacrifices for the relationship, and seeking professional support.

As Kathy and Kevin discovered, the path to recovery is not always easy. There may be setbacks, moments of doubt, and days when the pain feels as fresh as ever. But by staying committed to each other and the hard work of healing, they slowly began to rediscover the love, trust, and intimacy they had once shared - and to build a relationship that was even stronger and more authentic than before.

If you are currently navigating the aftermath of an affair, know that you are not alone. With courage, compassion, and a commitment to the journey, you can rekindle the love and trust in your relationship - one day, one step, one brave conversation at a time.

Chapter Twenty-One

Don't Trust Your Memory

The Insidious Impact of Denial and Distortion

When you've been betrayed by a partner's affair, the pain and confusion can be all-consuming, even to the point of obsession and overthinking. But when that betrayal is compounded by physical abuse, the trauma can take on an even more insidious form. In the aftermath of such a devastating experience, you may find yourself grappling not only with the shattered trust and heartbreak of infidelity but also with a distorted sense of reality that can leave you questioning your perceptions and memories.

This phenomenon, known as denial, is a common psychological defense mechanism that can arise in the face of trauma. When we experience something as profoundly painful and destabilizing as abuse and betrayal, our minds may seek to protect us by minimizing or distorting the severity of what happened. We may find ourselves doubting our own recollections, questioning whether things were as bad as they seemed, or even wondering if we somehow imagined or exaggerated the abuse.

It's a confusing and destabilizing experience that can leave you feeling like you're losing your grip on reality. You may find yourself replaying incidents in your mind, trying to make sense of what happened, only to have the details slip away or become muddied with each retelling. You may start to question whether you're overreacting or whether you somehow brought the abuse upon yourself.

This process of denial and distortion is particularly insidious because it can happen so gradually and subtly that you may not even realize it's occurring. As time passes and the immediate shock and pain of the betrayal begin to fade, your mind may start to engage in a kind of emotional airbrushing, smoothing over the rough edges of your memories and minimizing the impact of what you experienced.

It's important to understand that this is a normal and even adaptive response to trauma. Your mind is trying to protect you from the full weight of the pain and betrayal, to help you keep functioning in the face of an unbearable reality. But while this defense mechanism may provide some short-term relief, it can ultimately prevent you from fully processing and healing from the trauma.

That's why it's so crucial to take action as soon as possible, especially in the aftermath of an abusive affair. The longer you wait to confront the reality of what happened and seek support, the more time your mind has to engage in denial and distortion. This can make it increasingly difficult to trust your own perceptions and memories and to take the necessary steps to protect yourself and begin the process of healing.

One of the most powerful tools for combating denial and distortion is documentation. By keeping a detailed record of your experiences, emotions, and any physical evidence of abuse, you can create a tangible anchor that helps you stay grounded in reality. This might be a journal, a voice memo, or even photographs of any injuries or property damage.

When you write down what happened, you create an unambiguous record of the truth. You can refer back to this record whenever doubts or confusion start to creep in, reminding yourself that what you experienced was real and that your perceptions are valid. This documentation can also be invaluable if you decide to seek legal recourse or other forms of support in the future.

It's important to note that the phenomenon of denial and distortion can occur not only in cases of physical abuse but also in emotionally traumatic affairs where there is no overt violence. Gaslighting, manipulation, and other forms of psychological abuse can be just as damaging and disorienting as physical violence, leaving you doubting your instincts, perceptions, and what your gut is telling you. You may have numbed yourself to what you are being told. You may even be to the point of totally ignoring those warnings.

In these cases, trusting your gut and seeking outside support and validation is especially important. Talking to a trusted friend, family member, or therapist can help you gain perspective and clarity when your mind feels clouded by confusion and self-doubt. Surrounding yourself with people who believe in you and support you can be a powerful antidote to the isolating effects of denial and distortion.

Ultimately, healing from the trauma of an abusive affair is a journey that requires patience, self-compassion, and a commitment to facing the truth, even when it's painful. It's not an easy path, but it leads to greater clarity, strength, and resilience in the end.

If you're currently struggling with denial and distortion in the aftermath of an affair, know that you're not alone and that what you're experiencing is a normal response to an abnormal and traumatic situation. Reach out for help, whether it's to a trusted loved one, a therapist who specializes in trauma and betrayal, or a domestic violence support organization.

Your safety and well-being are paramount. Trust your instincts, even when your mind tries to convince you otherwise. Keep records, seek support, and hold onto the truth of your experience. With time, care, and compassion, you can begin to heal the wounds of betrayal and reclaim your sense of self and reality.

Safety is a priority. When you do not feel safe, your mind is not thinking straight and being rational. You become more reactive than rational. Only when you feel safe can you think through what is happening and start processing your emotions.

Resources:

- National Domestic Violence Hotline: 1-800-799-7233

- Betrayal Trauma Recovery, a support organization for survivors of betrayal and abuse: https://betrayaltraumarecovery.com/

Chapter Twenty-Two

The Pursuit of Details

How Seeking Information Can Hinder Intimacy

Pam sat across from her husband, Jonathan, her heart racing as she prepared to ask the question that had haunted her for weeks. "I need to know everything," she said, her voice trembling. "Every detail of the affair, every moment you spent with her. I can't move on until I have the full picture."

Jonathan shifted uncomfortably in his seat, his eyes filled with a mixture of guilt and apprehension. He knew Pam's request was coming from a place of deep pain and betrayal, but he also feared that rehashing every sordid detail would only deepen the wounds between them and hurt her more.

If you've found yourself in a situation like Pam and Jonathan's, grappling with the aftermath of an affair, you may be all too familiar with the overwhelming desire to uncover every aspect of your partner's betrayal. The need to know what happened, when, and with whom can feel like an obsession, a gnawing hunger that won't be satisfied until you have all the pieces of the puzzle.

But before you embark on a quest for information, it's essential to pause and ask yourself: What is driving this need? What do you hope to gain by knowing every intimate detail of the affair? And most importantly, will this knowledge truly bring you closer to healing and rebuilding the intimacy in your relationship?

I ask you this out of concern for you and the healing of your marriage. Consider whether or not that information will actually help with the healing of your marriage. One problem many individuals face later is, "How can I get those images and memories out of my head?" The fewer details you ask for now, the fewer memories you will struggle with later.

The truth is that the pursuit of details can often be a double edged sword. While some level of disclosure and honesty is undoubtedly necessary for rebuilding trust, an unhealthy fixation on the minutiae of the affair can hinder progress and deepen the emotional pain for both partners.

When we're in the throes of betrayal, it's natural to want to regain a sense of control over a situation that feels utterly chaotic and destabilizing. Gathering information may feel like piecing together the shattered fragments of our reality, trying to make sense of the unthinkable. We may hope that by understanding the full extent of the betrayal, we can somehow prevent it from happening again.

But the hard truth is that no amount of detail will ever fully explain or justify the affair. Knowing what positions they used or what gifts they exchanged won't erase the fact that it happened or magically restore the broken trust. Dwelling on these specifics can often lead to a dangerous cycle of rumination and obsession, where the past becomes an inescapable prison of pain.

As Pam discovered, the more she pressed Jonathan for details, the more distant and defensive he became. Instead of bringing them closer together, her interrogations only served to push them further apart. She found herself consumed by mental images of Jonathan's transgressions, replaying them over and over in her mind until she could barely stand to look at him without feeling sick.

What Pam and Jonathan needed wasn't more information but a new way of connecting and communicating. They needed to shift their focus from the sordid details of the affair to the underlying emotions, needs, patterns, and vulnerabilities that had led them to this point.

This is where the real work of affair recovery begins—not in the pursuit of facts but in the willingness to share one's deepest feelings and fears with honesty and vulnerability. It's about creating a safe, nonjudgmental space where both partners can express themselves authentically without fear of retribution, blame, or defensiveness.

For Jonathan, this meant being willing to take responsibility for the pain he had caused and to answer Pam's questions with patience and empathy. He had to find a way of directly answering her questions without excessive details. It meant being open about his own struggles and insecurities, even when they were uncomfortable or scary. Instead of telling her whether he enjoyed the experience or the attractiveness of his hook-up, he needed to talk about feeling a need for release and that he found someone willing to cater to his unhealthy desire.

For Pam, it meant learning to clearly communicate her needs and boundaries without resorting to accusations or demands. It meant being willing to listen to Jonathan's perspective with an open heart, even if it differed from hers. In her mind, she mapped out what he was thinking every step of the way and his motivations to the point that she was unwilling to hear from Jonathan what he was thinking. She had to set aside her preconceptions and hear him out.

Together, Pam and Jonathan began to focus on rebuilding their emotional intimacy through small, daily acts of connection and affection. They set aside time each day to check in with each other, share their feelings, and express gratitude for the efforts they were both making to heal their relationship.

They also sought the guidance of a skilled couples therapist who could help them navigate the complex emotions and challenges of affair recovery. With the support of their therapist, they learned new tools for communication, conflict resolution, and rebuilding trust.

Gradually, as they prioritized their emotional connection over the pursuit of details, Pam and Jonathan began to feel a new sense of closeness and understanding. They realized true intimacy wasn't about knowing every fact and figure of each other's lives but rather about being fully present and attuned to each other's hearts.

If you find yourself in a similar situation, caught in the trap of substituting information for intimacy, know that you are not alone. The pain and confusion you are experiencing are valid, and the desire for answers is understandable. But remember that the path to healing and reconnection lies not in the pursuit of details but in the willingness to share your deepest self with your partner and let go of fears and preconceptions.

Be patient with yourself and with the process. Seek support from trusted friends, family, or a qualified therapist who can offer guidance and perspective. Most importantly, don't lose sight of the ultimate goal - not to uncover every secret but to rebuild a relationship founded on honesty, empathy, and genuine intimacy.

With time, reduced defensiveness, setting aside preconceptions, being open to hearing what each other is saying, and a commitment to each other's healing, you can begin to move beyond the pain of the past and create a new, stronger bond—one built not on fragments of information but on the solid foundation of love, trust, and understanding.

Chapter Twenty-Three

Cheaters and Trust

Navigating the Challenges of Rebuilding Trust After an Affair

Katie and Tommy sat in their therapist's office, both feeling exhausted and overwhelmed. They had been working hard to rebuild their relationship after Tommy's affair, but it seemed like every time they made progress, something would set them back. Katie was frustrated with Tommy's resistance to some of the changes she felt were necessary to restore trust, while Tommy struggled with the constant reminders of his past mistakes.

Their story is not uncommon. When couples begin the difficult work of restoring their relationship after infidelity, they face numerous hurdles along the way. One of the first obstacles they must overcome is just being able to discuss the affair rationally. Once that foundation is laid, the couple can start tackling issues like forgiveness and rebuilding trust.

It's at this stage that many unfaithful partners begin to show the strongest resistance to change. Rebuilding trust leaves no room for secrecy or evasion - it requires complete transparency and accountability from the cheater. This can be a daunting prospect for someone who has grown accustomed to living a double life or compartmentalizing their behavior. Lying is a habit that does not go away without a fight.

There is also the hurdle of shame. Admitting what was done brings the issue of shame and guilt, which may have origins before the marriage.

If you're the betrayed partner, it's important not to be caught off guard by your unfaithful partner's resistance to rebuilding trust. They may drag their feet, make excuses, or even actively sabotage your efforts. This behavior can be incredibly frustrating and disheartening, but it's crucial to remember that it often stems from a place of fear, shame, and vulnerability.

Imagine how Tommy must have felt, knowing that rebuilding trust would require him to be an open book, to share every part of himself with Katie, even the parts he was deeply ashamed of. He was brought up being taught that "Some secrets you take to the grave." The prospect of being so exposed and vulnerable can be terrifying, especially for someone who has become accustomed to hiding and compartmentalizing parts of their life.

It's also common for cheaters to struggle with the weight of their own guilt and self-loathing. They may feel they don't deserve forgiveness or a second chance, leading them to push their partner away or resist fully engaging in the healing process. They may think, "What's the point? I'll just mess up again anyway," or "I don't deserve a happy marriage," or 'What makes you think change is possible?"

For Katie and Tommy, these dynamics created a push-and-pull that sometimes left them both feeling stuck and hopeless. But with the help of their therapist, they slowly began to understand and work through the underlying issues fueling Tommy's resistance.

One key realization was that rebuilding trust is not a quick or easy process. There is no magic solution or shortcut to repairing the damage caused by infidelity. Expecting things to return to "normal" after one heartfelt conversation or romantic gesture is unrealistic - real life doesn't work that way.

Instead, rebuilding trust requires consistent effort and demonstrable changes over time. It involves the cheater showing up day after day, making choices that prioritize their partner and the relationship, even when it's hard or uncomfortable.

Some signs that trust is gradually being earned and restored include:

1. The unfaithful partner follows through on their commitments and does what they say they will do.

2. They show dedication to the relationship, even when it requires personal sacrifices or discomfort.

3. The couple has more open, honest conversations about their thoughts, feelings, and needs without attacks or defensive reactions.

4. The unfaithful partner communicates without defensiveness or resentment, truly listening to and validating their partner's experiences.

5. They consider their partner's feelings and wishes more consistently when making decisions rather than only themselves.

6. The unfaithful partner shares information about their whereabouts, activities, and communications without being evasive or withholding.

7. They offer their partner open access to their devices, accounts, and financial information.

As Katie and Tommy worked to identify and celebrate these trust-building behaviors, they slowly felt more hopeful and connected. They learned to approach setbacks with compassion and understanding rather than accusation and blame.

Katie began to understand that Tommy's resistance wasn't a sign that he didn't love her or want to save their marriage but rather a manifestation of his own struggles and insecurities. She learned to balance holding him accountable with offering reassurance and support.

Tommy began to lean into the discomfort of being fully transparent, pushing through the shame and fear that held him back from being the partner Katie needed. He worked to replace defensiveness with empathy, to hear and acknowledge the pain his actions had caused.

Over time, with patience, persistence, and the support of their therapist, Katie and Tommy gradually rebuilt a stronger and more intimate foundation of trust than they had before. They discovered that by facing the challenges of infidelity head-on, with honesty and vulnerability, they could create a relationship built on genuine connection and understanding.

Chapter Twenty-Four

Rebuilding Trust After Infidelity

A Guide for Couples

Trust is the foundation of any healthy relationship, but when an affair shatters that trust, it can feel like an insurmountable obstacle to overcome. If you and your partner are committed to rebuilding your relationship after infidelity, understanding the key factors that influence trust can be a powerful tool in your healing journey.

Research has shown that trust is more readily granted and maintained when certain elements are present in a relationship. By cultivating these factors within your partnership, you can create an environment conducive to gradually restoring trust and intimacy.

Reliability and Follow-Through

One of the most critical components of trust is the belief that your partner has both the desire and the ability to follow through on their promises and commitments. In the wake of an affair, this can be particularly challenging, as the unfaithful partner's actions have directly contradicted their vows and eroded their credibility. Having the ability to follow through is especially important in situations involving brain traumas, where their abilities have been impaired.

To rebuild trust, the unfaithful partner must demonstrate a consistent pattern of reliability and follow-through. This means showing up physically and emotionally, keeping their word, and being accountable for their actions. It means making choices prioritizing the relationship and their partner's well-being, even when difficult or uncomfortable.

For example, if the unfaithful partner promises to attend couples therapy or to be home by a certain time, they must follow through on those commitments. Each kept promise, no matter how small, helps to rebuild a foundation of dependability and security.

Integrity and Honesty

Another key factor in rebuilding trust is the perception of honesty. Honesty is more than just telling the truth; it's about consistently aligning one's words and actions with one's values and principles. The degree to which what is said lines up with values and principles is integrity. When an affair occurs, it represents a major breach of integrity, as the unfaithful partner has violated the core values of honesty, loyalty, and commitment that are central to a healthy relationship.

To repair this breach, the unfaithful partner must be willing to take a hard look at their behavior and make a genuine effort to live with integrity moving forward. This involves being transparent about their thoughts, feelings, and actions, even when it's uncomfortable or exposes their vulnerabilities. It means being honest about the affair itself, answering questions openly and without defensiveness, and taking full responsibility for the pain they have caused.

It's important to note that rebuilding integrity takes time and consistent effort. The betrayed partner may need ongoing reassurance and evidence of their partner's commitment to honesty before they can begin to fully trust again. This is a natural part of the healing process and should be approached with patience and understanding.

Commitment

Finally, trust is more easily fostered in a relationship where both partners display genuine care and concern for each other's well-being and are committed to your relationship. When we feel seen, heard, and valued by our partners who are committed to the relationship, we are more likely to feel safe being vulnerable and open with them.

In the context of healing from infidelity, both partners can work to cultivate an atmosphere of commitment. The unfaithful partner can show commitment by being attuned to their partner's feelings, actively listening to their concerns, and responding with empathy and validation. Let them know you are committed to them, no matter how uncomfortable you feel. They can demonstrate their commitment to the relationship through small acts of thoughtfulness, affection, and support.

While understandably hurt and angry, the betrayed partner can also contribute to a commitment by expressing their needs and boundaries clearly and compassionately and letting them know you are not giving up. They can work to manage their own emotional reactivity and approach conflicts with a spirit of goodwill and a desire for understanding.

Each spouse needs to know that the other is committed to the relationship. They need the reassurance that disagreements do not equate to ending the relationship. They need to know that each other will be there for each other.

Patience, Persistence, and Professional Support

It's important to remember that rebuilding trust after an affair is a gradual and often challenging process. There will likely be setbacks, moments of doubt and discouragement, and times when progress feels slow or stalled. This is a normal and understandable part of the journey, and both partners need to approach the process with patience and realistic expectations.

Some days, it may feel like you're taking two steps forward and one step back. On other days, the pain of the betrayal may feel as fresh and raw as ever. During these times, it's crucial to lean on your support systems, whether that's trusted friends and family, a support group, or a qualified therapist who specializes in helping couples heal from infidelity.

A skilled therapist can provide a safe, neutral space for you and your partner to process your emotions, develop effective communication strategies, and work through the complex challenges of rebuilding trust. They can offer guidance and perspective that can be difficult to access when you're in the midst of such a painful and emotionally charged situation.

Ultimately, rebuilding trust after an affair requires a deep commitment from both partners to do the hard work of self-reflection, honest communication, and consistent, trust-building action. It requires a willingness to confront painful truths, to take responsibility for one's own healing, and to extend empathy and forgiveness even when it feels unnatural or undeserved.

Chapter Twenty-Five

Embracing the Journey Ahead

A Path to Healing, Growth, and Renewed Love

As you reach the end of this book, you've gained valuable insights and understanding about the complex nature of affairs, their impact on relationships, and the process of rebuilding trust and intimacy in the aftermath of betrayal. You now stand at a crossroads, equipped with knowledge but perhaps still feeling uncertain about how to translate that knowledge into action.

Taking the First Step: A Reflective Exercise

As you embark on this journey of healing and growth, it's important to start by clarifying your intentions and commitments. Take a few moments to reflect on the following questions:

1. What are your primary goals for your relationship moving forward?
2. What specific actions can you take today to achieve those goals?

3. How can you prioritize self-care and seek support during this challenging time?

Write down your answers in a journal or discuss them with your partner or a trusted friend. By articulating your intentions and identifying concrete steps you can take, you'll be better prepared to face the challenges ahead.

Navigating Setbacks and Maintaining Momentum

It's important to remember that the path to recovery is rarely a straight line. There will likely be moments of progress and joy, as well as setbacks and disappointments. This is a normal part of the healing process, and it's crucial to approach these challenges with patience, self-compassion, and a commitment to ongoing growth.

When you encounter obstacles or setbacks, remember to:

1. Acknowledge and validate your emotions without judgment

2. Reach out for support from loved ones, a therapist, or a support group

3. Focus on the progress you've made rather than dwelling on temporary setbacks

4. Recommit to your goals and values as individuals and as a couple

By maintaining a growth mindset and a willingness to learn from challenges, you'll be better equipped to navigate the ups and downs of the recovery journey.

Seeking Support and Prioritizing Self-Care

As you rebuild your relationship, don't forget to prioritize your own emotional and physical well-being. Engaging in regular self-care practices, such as exercise, mindfulness, or creative pursuits, can help you build resilience and maintain a positive outlook in the face of stress.

Self-care also includes healthy eating. Skipping meals or eating unhealthy food impacts your mental and emotional functioning, leaving you in a state of reacting with a 'fight, flight, or freeze' response. Recovery from an affair requires you to be rational and able to tune into your partner along with your own emotions and thoughts.

It's also essential to seek support from others who understand what you're going through. Consider reaching out to trusted friends or family members, joining a support group for couples affected by infidelity, or working with a qualified therapist who specializes in affair recovery.

Remember, you don't have to face this challenge alone. By surrounding yourself with a supportive network and prioritizing your own healing, you'll be better equipped to show up fully and compassionately in your relationship.

The Power of Hope and Resilience

The journey ahead may be difficult sometimes, but it is also an opportunity for profound growth, healing, and transformation. You have within you the strength, resilience, and capacity to rebuild a stronger, more authentic, and more deeply connected relationship than ever before.

By committing to the hard work of recovery, practicing patience and self-compassion, and seeking the support you need, you can emerge from this challenge with a renewed sense of purpose and a deeper appreciation for the love you share.

Embracing the Journey Ahead

As you turn the final pages of this book, I encourage you to take the first step towards healing and growth. Reflect on your goals, prioritize self-care, and seek the support you need to navigate the challenges ahead.

Remember, healing is possible. Happiness is possible. And you are worthy of both.

Trust in the journey ahead, knowing you are moving closer to the fulfilling, joyful relationship you deserve with each step forward. Embrace the opportunity for growth and transformation, and have faith in your ability to create a brighter future together.

Your journey of healing and renewal begins now. May you find strength, compassion, and unwavering hope as you embark on this transformative path towards a more loving, trusting, and deeply connected relationship.

About The Author

As a teenager, I experienced the devastation caused by infidelity first-hand when my family went through a parental affair. Navigating through the aftermath, which involved children's protective services, domestic abuse, legal fights, and emotional upheaval, left me feeling helpless and alone.

Determined to learn from these experiences, I became a Licensed Professional Counselor (LPC) and Licensed Chemical Dependency Counselor (LCDC). For over 40 years, I have helped thousands of families across various settings, applying an approach founded on proven Biblical principles and neuropsychology discoveries.

As an early pioneer in online counseling, I have been helping people through articles, e-books, and telephone sessions since 1999. My work has been featured on Wall Street Journal Radio, the Larry Elder Show, and numerous other media.

Married since 1985, my wife Peggy and I have been blessed with three incredible sons. We have navigated the challenges and temptations in our own marriage, and I am committed to helping others overcome the pain of affairs and rebuild their relationships.

You may contact me via email at jeff@restorethefamily.com.

Follow me on Medium @RestoreTheFamily

Receive my daily newsletter at www.SurviveYourPartnersAffair.com

The Affair Recovery Workhop
Transform Your Marriage

Are you ready to embark on a transformative journey to heal your marriage and rediscover the love, trust, and intimacy you once shared? The Affair Recovery Workshop, created by renowned relationship expert Jeffrey D. Murrah, LPC, LCDC, is your essential companion to this book, offering a unique and comprehensive approach to navigating the complex emotions and challenges that follow infidelity. With a proven track record of success and a personalized approach tailored to your needs, this workshop provides you with the in-depth guidance, interactive experience, and practical tools necessary to rebuild a stronger, more resilient relationship.

Why the Affair Recovery Workshop is the Essential Companion to this Book

1. In-depth Guidance: While the book lays a solid foundation for understanding infidelity and the recovery process, the video program dives deeper into the critical topics, offering 2.5 hours of expert guidance from Jeffrey D. Murrah. The extended format allows for a more thorough exploration of the strategies and techniques needed to rebuild trust, improve communication, and foster intimacy.

2. Interactive Experience: The video program provides an engaging and interactive learning experience that complements the book. With visual aids, real-life examples, and guided exercises, you can actively apply the concepts and strategies to your own situation, enhancing your understanding and retention of the material.

3. Personalized Approach: The Affair Recovery Workshop recognizes that every couple's situation is unique. The video program offers a personalized approach, helping you identify and address your relationship's specific challenges and dynamics. This targeted guidance can accelerate healing and lead to more effective outcomes.

4. Convenient and Flexible: With 24/7 access to the video modules, a comprehensive 68-page workbook, and a bonus ebook, "How Can I Trust You Again?", you can work through the program at your own pace, from the privacy and comfort of your own home. This flexibility ensures you can fully engage with the content and implement the strategies on your own terms.

Real Testimonials from Transformed Lives

"The Affair Recovery Workshop was the turning point in our healing journey. Jeffrey's in-depth guidance and personalized approach helped us navigate the complex emotions and rebuild our marriage stronger than ever." - Sarah and Michael, married 9 years.

"The interactive experience of the video program, combined with the practical exercises in the workbook, allowed us to dive deeper into understanding and addressing the unique challenges in our relationship. It was a game-changer for us." - Lisa and David, married 14 years.

Your Journey to a Stronger Marriage Starts Here

Invest in your marriage and your future happiness with the **Affair Recovery Workshop**. As a special offer exclusively available through this book, we're extending a 30% discount on the workshop to help you start your transformative journey. Visit **www.AffairRecoveryWorkshop.com** and use the coupon code **WORKSHOP30** to claim your discount. This limited-time offer is our commitment to your success.

Don't let infidelity define your marriage. Take the first step towards healing and renewal today, and give yourself the best opportunity to achieve the transformation you seek. With our 30-day unconditional guarantee, you have nothing to lose and everything to gain.

What You'll Receive:

- In-depth video modules (2.5 hours of expert guidance)
    - 68-page comprehensive workbook
    - Bonus ebook: "How Can I Trust You Again?"
    - 24/7 access to the program
    - 30-day unconditional guarantee
    - Strictly confidential participation

By combining the insights from the book with the immersive experience of the Affair Recovery Workshop, you'll be equipped with the knowledge, tools, and support needed to overcome the devastation of infidelity and build a stronger, more resilient marriage.

Take action now and claim your 30% discount on the Affair Recovery Workshop. Visit **www.AffairRecoveryWorkshop.com** and use the coupon code **WORKSHOP30** to start your transformative journey today. Your satisfaction is 100% guaranteed.

Wishing you all the best on your path to healing and rediscovering the love and connection you deserve,

Jeffrey D. Murrah, LPC, LCDC

www.ingramcontent.com/pod-product-compliance
Lightning Source LLC
Chambersburg PA
CBHW071338140726
47996CB00005B/2034